Reading & Writing *Excellence*

KEYS TO STANDARDS-BASED ASSESSMENT

Carol Alexander

STECK-VAUGHN
BERRENT
A Harcourt Company

www.steck-vaughn.com

ACKNOWLEDGMENTS

Project Author: Carol Alexander

Executive Editor: Carol Traynor

Senior Editor: Amy Losi

Editor II: Caren Churchbuilder

Editor I: Edward Nasello

Associate Editor: Christy Yaros

Project Consultant: Howard Berrent

Art Director: Frank Bruno

Design and Production: Susan Geer Associates, Inc.

Designer I: Julene Mays

Design Associate: Gregory Silverman

Cover Design: S. Michelle Wiggins

Photo Research: Sarah Fraser

Illustrators: Eva Cockrille

Eileen Hine

CD Hullinger

Holly Jones

Steck-Vaughn/Berrent is indebted to the following for permission to use material in this book:

page 9 "Moving Blues" by Kelly Musselman. Copyright © 2001 by Highlights for Children, Inc., Columbus, Ohio.

page 24 "Are Animals Inventors?" by Gail Jarrow and Paul Sherman. Copyright © 2001 by Highlights for Children, Inc., Columbus, Ohio.

page 34 "The Dust-Colored Coyote" adapted by Gay Seltzer. Copyright © 2001 by Highlights for Children, Inc., Columbus, Ohio.

page 46 "Who Was Peter Pan?" – Reprinted by permission of CRICKET magazine, May 2001, Vol. 28, No. 9, © 2001 by Kristina Cliff-Evans.

page 50 "A Boy and a Man" from BANNER IN THE SKY. Copyright 1954, by James Ramsey Ullman. Used by permission of HarperCollins Publishers.

page 58 "Tyrannosaurus Sue." Infoplease.com. © 2001 Learning Network. http://www.infoplease.com/ipa/A0873492.html (6/27/01)

page 82 "Amaterasu, the Sun Goddess" adapted by Matt Evans. Courtesy of AFRO-AMERICAN NEWSPAPERS ARCHIVES AND RESEARCH CENTER.

Photo Credits:
p.25 ©Richard Kolar/Animals Animals; p.30 ©Reuters New Media Inc./CORBIS; p.38 ©Stephen Trimble/DRK Photo; p.46 ©Bettmann/CORBIS; p.47 ©Jeremy Horner/CORBIS; p.58 ©Reuters New Media Inc./CORBIS; p.70 ©Bettmann/ CORBIS

Additional photography by: Getty and Steck Vaughn Collection

STECK-VAUGHN BERRENT

A Harcourt Company

www.steck-vaughn.com

ISBN 0-7398-3955-1

Copyright © 2002 Steck-Vaughn Company

Published by Steck-Vaughn/Berrent Publications, a division of Steck-Vaughn Company.

1 2 3 4 5 6 7 8 9 TPO 06 05 04 03 02

Table of Contents

Students are instructed to approach a selection and test question using the **Four *R*s:** **R**eady, **R**ead, **R**espond, **R**eview.

Unit 1 introduces the three levels of comprehension—literal, interpretive, and critical—and presents specific strategies designed to assist students in answering multiple-choice and short-answer questions. Each question is identified in the instruction by the type of skill it covers.

Unit 2 explains how students can use graphic organizers to help them answer essay questions. A graphic organizer accompanies each of six selections. Students are given instruction in how to use the different organizers to answer essay questions about the selections. Each question is identified in the instruction by the type of skill it covers.

Unit 3 builds upon what was taught in the previous two units. Students apply what they have learned to answer multiple-choice and open-ended questions about various selections. There are hints to help them answer each question. Each question is identified in the hint by the type of skill it covers.

Unit 4 provides students with an opportunity to independently practice the strategies they have learned. This unit may be used as a test to assess students' learning and to simulate formal tests.

To the Teacher

Reading & Writing Excellence is a series of instructional books designed to prepare students to take standardized reading tests. It introduces the **Four *R*s,** a strategy that will enable students to read selections, understand what they have read, and answer multiple-choice and open-ended questions about the reading material. Special emphasis is given to using graphic organizers as prewriting aids for answering essay questions.

Many genres, such as fiction, nonfiction, poems, fables, and folk tales are included. Some of the passages are taken from published literature, reflecting the type of instruction that exists in classrooms today. The questions accompanying each passage represent the different levels of comprehension.

The material in this book provides your students with step-by-step instruction that will maximize their reading success in classroom work as well as in testing situations.

The Four *R*s to Success

When you approach any kind of a task, it helps to start with a plan. A plan provides you with the specific steps you must follow to accomplish your goal.

When you take a reading test, you need a plan that will help you understand a selection and answer questions about it. You can follow this plan by remembering the **Four *R*s:** **R**eady, **R**ead, **R**espond, **R**eview.

Ready   Before you read, you need to get ready.

▶ **Set a purpose for reading**   Think about why you are reading. This will help you to focus. If you are reading to answer questions for a test, you will be looking for information. You will also be reading to understand how the different parts of the selection fit together.

▶ **Preview the selection**   Try to find out as much about the selection as you can before you read it. Read the title, flip through the pages, glance at any illustrations or diagrams, and read any headings. You might also want to skim the first paragraph.

▶ **Make predictions**   Next, predict what you will find in the text.

Read   The next step is to read the selection. You will better understand what you read if you take an active role.

▶ **Anticipate what will follow**   Continue to make predictions as you work your way through the text. For works of fiction, ask yourself, "What will happen next?" For nonfiction selections, try to figure out what the next part of the selection will be about.

▶ **Monitor your own understanding**   As you read, ask yourself questions about things you might not understand. Take the time to speculate about answers to your questions. Then, reread parts of the selection to determine if your answers are correct.

▶ **Confirm your predictions**   Keep your predictions in mind as you read. Are things turning out the way you expected? Make new predictions as you acquire more information. Continue the process until you have finished the selection.

Respond Now you are ready to answer some questions about the selection.

▶ **Read the question** Read each question carefully. For multiple-choice questions, be sure to read each of the choices as well.

▶ **Think about it** Think about which parts of the selection will help you figure out the answer. Reread those sections. For multiple-choice questions, have the choices in mind as you do this. For open-ended questions, be sure to organize your thoughts before you begin to write your answer.

▶ **Answer the question** You are now ready to answer the question. For multiple-choice questions, more than one answer often sounds right. Be careful to choose the *best* answer. If you are writing your answer, make sure to include all the points you want to make.

Review Take another look at your answer. Did you pick the best choice for your multiple-choice question? Did you answer all parts of your open-ended question? Does your answer make sense? Be sure to check your spelling, punctuation, and grammar.

• • •

UNIT 1

Three Levels of Comprehension

In this unit you will learn how to answer questions at three "key" levels of comprehension.

LEVEL 1: *Find the Key* (Literal Level)

Look for information—At the literal level, you recall or recognize information. The information you need is stated right in the selection.

LEVEL 2: *Turn the Lock* (Interpretive Level)

Determine meaning—At the interpretive level, you use the information in the selection to figure out the answers to questions. You might be explaining meaning. Or, you might be using clues to draw conclusions. For this level, you must show that you understand the information in the selection. You must also know how the different parts fit together.

LEVEL 3: *Open the Door* (Critical Level)

Go beyond the text—At the critical level, you think about the selection and add what you know from your own experiences. You evaluate and extend meaning. You also make judgments about what you have read.

LEVEL 1: Find the Key
Introduction to Literal Questions

A literal question will ask you to recall or recognize information that is directly stated in the passage.

Types of literal questions may include the following:

► Identifying details from the selection

► Identifying the order of events

► Identifying cause-and-effect situations

► Identifying character traits

Identify key words

The key to answering a literal question is to find out where the answer is located. Think about where the information might appear in the selection. Then identify key words in the question that might also appear in the passage. For example, look at the following question:

What types of common houseplants are poisonous?

To answer this question, you would look for the key words *common*, *houseplants*, and *poisonous*. If you cannot find these words, look for words that mean about the same thing. Instead of *poisonous*, for example, you might look for *toxic* or *deadly*. Or, you might look for examples of harmful effects from plants, such as *skin rashes* or *illness*.

Find the clues

Sometimes you will not have key words to help you. Then you must think carefully about what the question is asking. Look at this question:

Which sentence states the main idea of the passage?

Here there are no key words to look for, but the answer can still be found in the selection. First, you must know that the *main idea* is the central idea in the passage. So you would look for the one sentence that clearly tells what the whole selection is about.

Answering Literal Questions

Now you will learn how to answer literal questions about a story. Be sure to follow the **Four R**s:

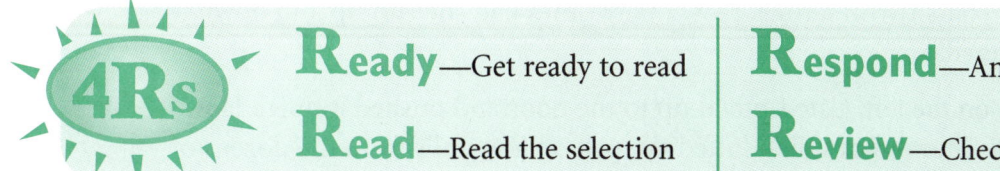

4Rs   **R**eady—Get ready to read   **R**espond—Answer the question
            Read—Read the selection   **R**eview—Check your answer

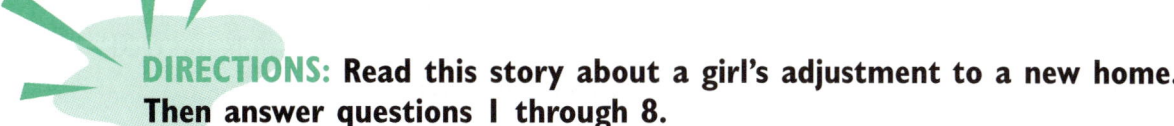

DIRECTIONS: Read this story about a girl's adjustment to a new home. Then answer questions I through 8.

Moving Blues

by Kelly Musselman

Cate walked slowly through the empty house one more time. "Good-bye, kitchen," she whispered. A shiny spot on the scuffed linoleum stood out where the refrigerator had been until yesterday afternoon.

Dark squares stood out on the living room walls where family pictures had hung. Cate rubbed her sneaker over a pink stain in the carpet. That was where she'd spilled a glass of grape juice when she was seven. The stain never did come out, and her mother ended up moving the furniture around to hide it.

Cate's throat tightened when she passed the door to the laundry room. Short lines were pencilled across the door frame, with tiny numbers written next to them. Cate ran a finger over the numbers as she read them out loud.

"Age two, thirty-four inches. Age three, thirty-eight inches. Age four, forty inches. Age five, forty-four inches."

"Stand up straight, now," her dad would say as she stood against the wall. Then he'd place the ruler on her head and mark the frame with his pencil. "No fair stretching!" he'd say with a laugh.

Cate sighed. Whoever bought the house would just paint over the numbers. All the growing up she'd done here wouldn't mean anything to them.

"Cate! We're almost ready to leave. Do you have everything?"

Cate jumped, startled. "Um, yes, I guess so, Dad. I just wanted to see my room one more time before we go."

"All right, but hurry up."

Cate took the stairs two at a time. How many times had she run up and down these stairs, she wondered.

Second room on the left. Cate tiptoed up to the door and pushed it open. How lifeless it looked! Thumbtack holes dotted the pale yellow walls from the dozens of posters she'd hung up over the years.

She gazed out the window at the yard below. There was her jungle gym, bare patches under the swings where she'd dragged her feet a thousand times. Her old sandbox, which her mother had turned into an herb garden. Her favorite tree to climb and read books in. How many hours had she spent daydreaming there?

Cate pressed her cheek against the window, her breath fogging the glass. Well, it was no use daydreaming now, she thought, blinking back tears. They were moving, and there was nothing she could do about it. The only thing she was sure about was that she didn't like it.

• • •

"So, what do you think?" Mom asked.

"It's OK." Cate shrugged.

"OK? Just OK? Why, I think it's the nicest one we've looked at."

"Not as nice as our old house," Cate mumbled under her breath.

Mom pulled her into a hug. "Cate, I know you miss our old house, but we can't go back to it. Dad's job is here now."

Cate wriggled out of her mother's grasp. She stood by the fireplace and stared into the cold ashes.

"Why don't you take a look outside while I talk with the real-estate agent?" Mom suggested.

Cate sighed and trudged out the front door, banging it noisily behind her. The yard was big, with lots of old oak trees that stretched their branches up to the second-floor windows. Cate noticed that one huge gnarled oak had crooked wooden steps nailed up the side of it.

She clambered up the oak. On the second-to-last step, her foot slipped as the board wobbled to the right. "Oomph," she gasped as she grabbed for the last rung. Down was a long way off, and she didn't want to fall. She pulled herself into the crook of the tree.

"Not bad," she said, looking around. The leaves were thick, but she had a clear view of the house and the property below. She could see into one of the upstairs bedrooms.

From here she could probably even climb in! She leaned closer to the window.

The pane was smudged, but she could see an empty room with a dusty wooden floor and a window seat. There were two doors, one of which she figured must lead to a closet.

Cate settled back in the tree. A large knothole in the opposite limb caught her eye. Maybe it was a squirrel's home. Hanging on to a limb, Cate stood up to peek inside. There was something in the hole, but it wasn't a squirrel.

Cate reached in and pulled out a metal tube. On a piece of tape stuck to the side were written the words *The Will of Ellen Cartwright. Open only if you seek adventure!*

Cate carefully sat down in the crook of the oak. She screwed the top off the tube and with trembling fingers pulled out a rolled-up piece of paper.

"Dear Adventurous One: I call you that because I figure that if you have found this will, then you managed to survive the wobbly second-to-last step on this tree. (I kept meaning to fix that!)

"Now I shall tell you what I, Ellen Cartwright, bequeath to you in this will.

"First, I leave you my room. You can see it from this very spot, and yes, you can climb into it from this tree—if the window is open, that is!

"I leave you my window seat for reading, thinking, and bird-watching (it's the best spot in the house) and the big walk-in closet for playing, hiding, and throwing all your stuff into when your mom tells you to clean your room.

"I leave you the banister on the stairs for sliding down, the fireplace for roasting marshmallows, and a front door that bangs really loud. I also leave you the basketball hoop in the driveway, the blackberry (yummy!) bushes in the backyard, and of course, this wonderful old tree.

"I've lived here all my life, and leaving this house was one of the hardest things I've had to do. The only things I can't leave you are the memories that I made here; I took them with me. But I know that you won't need them. You'll be busy making your own.

"So, I leave you. I am off seeking new memories at my new home.

"Ellen Cartwright, age 12."

Cate rolled up the note, slipped it back into the metal tube, and stuck the tube into her pocket. "The first thing I'm going to do," she said as she climbed down from the oak, "is to fix that wobbly step." After all, this was going to be her tree now. Ellen had left it to her, the Adventurous One.

DIRECTIONS: Read each question carefully. Darken the circle at the bottom of the page or write your answer on the lines.

1 Cate had to leave her old house because—

A her family needed a bigger house

B her father found a new job

C her family was moving in with her grandparents

D her old house was going to be torn down

Find the Key

This question asks you to identify details from the story. Read the question and the choices carefully. The answer to this question is right in the story. Think about where it might be found. Look for key words in the story that have to do with *why* the family moved.

2 The boxes show some things that happen in the story.

Cate goes to say goodbye to her bedroom in the old house.		Cate discovers a metal tube in the oak tree by the house.
1	2	3

Which event belongs in Box 2?

F Cate decides to fix the step leading up to the old tree.

G Cate wanders around the kitchen of the old house.

H Cate pulls herself into the crook of an old oak tree.

J Cate reads *The Will of Ellen Cartwright.*

Find the Key

This question asks you to identify the sequence of events in the story. Go back to the story and find each event in the boxes. Then read each choice to see which event occurs *between* the two in the boxes.

Answers

1 Ⓐ Ⓑ Ⓒ Ⓓ   **2** Ⓕ Ⓖ Ⓗ Ⓙ

3 The marks on the wall in the laundry room in Cate's old house show—

   A how old Cate is

   B how many people have lived there

   C how tall Cate has grown

   D how often Cate has washed clothes

Find the Key

Here you must also identify details. The question asks you to tell the purpose of the marks on the wall. Go back to the part of the story that tells about Cate's old house. Find when she walks to the laundry room. What do the marks on the wall show?

4 Cate is able to see her new room when she—

   F opens a second door

   G steps on a blackberry bush

   H reads a note in a bottle

   J climbs an old oak tree

Find the Key

Identify details from the story. This question asks you to tell how Cate can see her new room. Skim the story to find the part where Cate looks into her new room. Where is she when she does this? How is she able to see the room?

Answers

3 Ⓐ Ⓑ Ⓒ Ⓓ	4 Ⓕ Ⓖ Ⓗ Ⓙ

5 Who is Ellen Cartwright? Give some details from the story.

_____

_____

_____

_____

Find the Key

This question asks you to identify a character. Now, instead of choosing an answer, you will be writing your own answer to a question. Read the question carefully. Find the part of the story where Ellen Cartwright is mentioned. Who is she? Write your answer in a complete sentence.

6 How does Cate's old room look when she sees it for the last time?

_____

_____

_____

_____

Find the Key

Here you must identify details about a particular setting in the story. The answer is right in the story. Find the section in which Cate takes one last look at her room. What does she see? Pay attention to the descriptive words that are used in this part. You will find the answer here.

7   How does Cate feel about her new house when she first sees it? Why does she feel this way?

_____

_____

_____

_____

Find the Key

Here you must identify character traits. You must describe how Cate feels about something. The answer is in the story. Go back to the part where Cate's mother asks her what she thinks of the new house. What does Cate say? How does she feel about moving into it? Write your answer in a complete sentence.

8   Why does Ellen Cartwright leave a will in the tree?

_____

_____

_____

_____

Find the Key

This question also asks you to identify character traits and find details in the story. Reread the part of the story that discusses Ellen's will. The sentences within the quotation marks contain this information. Read this part of the story again. Then, in a sentence or two tell why Ellen leaves a will in the old tree.

LEVEL 2: Turn the Lock
Introduction to Interpretive Questions

To solve a mystery, a detective puts together clues to determine the guilty party. When you answer an interpretive question, you put together different pieces of information from a selection to determine its meaning.

Types of interpretive questions may include the following:

► Interpreting character traits

► Interpreting vocabulary

► Determining the main idea

► Summarizing information

► Drawing conclusions

Unlock the answer

To answer an interpretive question, you must become a detective. Before a detective can look for clues, he or she must know what to look for. You can tell what to look for by examining the question.

Suppose you had to answer a question about a chapter from *The Adventures of Tom Sawyer* by Mark Twain. In the chapter, young Tom tricks his friends into helping him paint a fence. Look at the following question:

**What character traits help Tom convince
his friends to help him paint the fence?**

The narrator or another person in a work of fiction might tell you what a character is like. More often, however, you will have to infer the character's traits by looking carefully at what he or she thinks, says, and does. What sections of the chapter might you reread to help you? You could look at the conversations that Tom has with his friends. You could also consider Tom's actions and what he is thinking while he carries out his scheme.

Put the clues together

After you have reread parts of the selection, think about what you have read. Then, like a detective, put the clues together to draw a conclusion.

For the question above, you might find that Tom is clever, imaginative, and manipulative. All of these traits help Tom trick his friends.

Answering Interpretive Questions

Now you will learn how to answer interpretive questions about a poem. Remember to follow the **Four Rs:**

4Rs

Ready—Get ready to read

Read—Read the selection

Respond—Answer the question

Review—Check your answer

DIRECTIONS: Read this poem about a place that remains the same only in memories. Then answer questions I through 8.

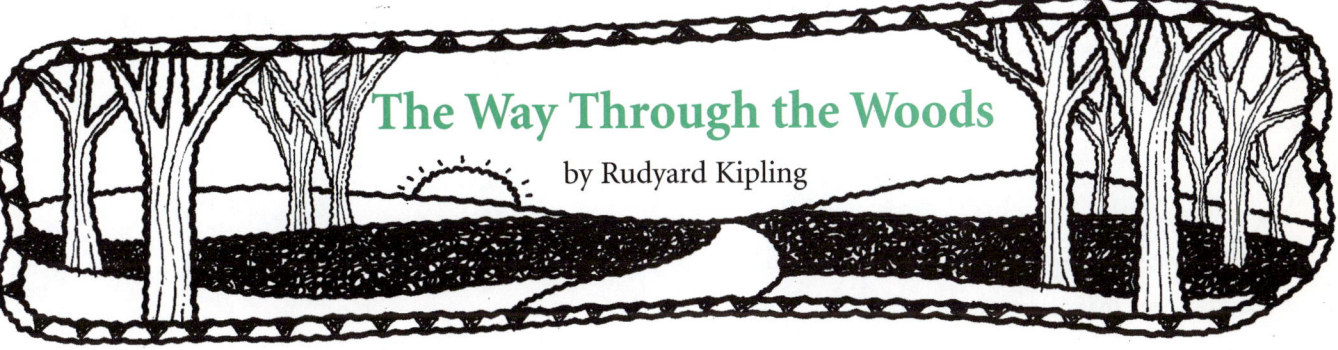

The Way Through the Woods
by Rudyard Kipling

They shut the road through the woods
Seventy years ago.
Weather and rain have *undone* it again,
And now you would never know
There was once a road through the woods
Before they planted the trees.
It is underneath the **coppice and heath,**
And the thin **anemones.**
Only the keeper sees
That, where the ring-dove broods,
And the badgers roll at ease,
There was once a road through the woods.

Yet, if you enter the woods
Of a summer evening late,
When the night-air cools on the trout-ringed pools
Where the otter whistles his mate,
(They fear not men in the woods,
Because they see so few.)
You will hear the beat of a horse's feet,
And the swish of a skirt in the dew,
Steadily cantering through
The misty solitudes,
As though they perfectly knew
The old lost road through the woods…
But there is no road through the woods.

coppice and heath: land covered with shrubs and plants
anemones: types of flowers

DIRECTIONS: Read each question carefully. Darken the circle at the bottom of the page or write your answer on the lines.

1   What does the word *undone* mean in this poem?

   A   discovered

   B   abandoned

   C   built

   D   destroyed

Turn the Lock

This is a vocabulary question. The word *undone* may be new to you, but you can figure it out from the words around it. The prefix *un* should also give you a clue. Reread the part of the poem that has the word *undone*. Does it give you any clues to the meaning of the word? What would most likely happen to a road that no one used anymore?

2   What is the theme of the poem?

   F   Never leave a stone unturned.

   G   The past lives in our memories.

   H   It is wrong to fight nature.

   J   No one can predict the future.

Turn the Lock

The question asks you to determine the theme of the poem. The theme of a poem or a story is the author's message. The theme is usually not stated, so you can't go back and find it. You have to look for clues in the writing and determine what the author is trying to say. Reread the poem and think about what the author is saying. Look at the answer choices. Which one best tells the theme of the poem?

Answers

1 Ⓐ Ⓑ Ⓒ Ⓓ	2 Ⓕ Ⓖ Ⓗ Ⓙ

3 Which word *best* tells how the speaker feels about the old road?

    A fond

    B scared

    C angry

    D excited

Turn the Lock

This question asks for a word that describes the speaker's feelings or point of view. When choosing an answer, think about the mood of the poem. How does the speeker seem to feel about the road? How would he sound if he were speaking?

4 What is this poem *mostly* about?

    F Animals on a road on a summer evening

    G A road that used to travel through the woods

    H A keeper who cares for an old road

    J Trees that have grown over a road in the woods

Turn the Lock

This question asks you to identify the main idea of the poem, or what the poem is mostly about. Reread the poem and the answer choices. Choose the answer choice that tells what the entire poem is about, not just a detail in the poem.

Answers

3 Ⓐ Ⓑ Ⓒ Ⓓ	4 Ⓕ Ⓖ Ⓗ Ⓙ

5 What has happened to the road since it was closed seventy years ago?

_____

_____

_____

_____

Turn the Lock

In this question, you must determine the meaning of the poem. Reread the beginning of the poem. What has happened to the road? Why does the speaker say "And now you would never know / There was once a road through the woods"?

6 Read these lines from the poem.

> **You will hear the beat of a horse's feet,**
> **And the swish of a skirt in the dew,**
> **Steadily cantering through**
> **The misty solitudes,**

What does the speaker mean by these lines?

_____

_____

_____

_____

Turn the Lock

Here you are asked to interpret the language of the poem and determine what it means. To answer this question, you need to think about the meaning of the poem. What has happened to the old road? Why does the speaker say you can hear these things? How does he hear them?

7 What can you tell about the speaker of the poem?

_____

_____

_____

_____

Turn the Lock

This question asks you to determine character traits. The answer to this question is not stated in the poem. Reread the poem and look for clues. Think about how the speaker feels. What can you tell about him from the poem?

8 Write a sentence or two that summarizes the poem.

_____

_____

_____

_____

Turn the Lock

This question asks you to summarize the poem. When you summarize, you do not simply retell what happened. You include only the most important points. Reread the poem. What are the most important points?

LEVEL 3: Open the Door
Introduction to Critical Questions

For a critical question, you must go beyond the words on the page. You bring in your own experiences to evaluate, extend meaning, and make judgments about what you have read.

Types of critical questions may include the following:

► Analyzing the situation

► Predicting outcomes

► Determining the author's purpose

► Extending the passage

► Evaluating the passage

Step through the door

Now, you are going to play the role of a judge. Although you will still look for clues to answer a question, now you must also study the information, decide on its importance, and make judgments about it.

Let's go back to the chapter from *The Adventures of Tom Sawyer*. Look at this question:

What do you think should happen to Tom after the chapter ends?

There is no way to find the answer in the story. Even putting together clues will not give you the answer. This question is asking for your opinion. You must base this opinion on what has happened in the story and on your own experiences.

Make a case

A judge never makes a hasty decision, and neither should you. First, consider what you know about the story. To trick the boys, Tom makes painting a fence seem like fun. The boys are so impressed that they bribe Tom to let them do his work for him.

Next, consider how you feel about Tom's actions. Do you see anything wrong with what Tom did? Or, do you think he deserves credit for getting others to do his work?

Now you can make a judgment on what should happen to Tom, based on the story and your feelings about the situation.

Answering Critical Questions

Now you will learn how to answer critical questions about two passages. Don't forget to follow the **Four *R*s:**

4Rs

***R*eady**—Get ready to read

***R*ead**—Read the selection

***R*espond**—Answer the question

***R*eview**—Check your answer

DIRECTIONS: Read this article about an intelligent animal. Next, read "Are Animals Inventors?" Then answer questions 1 and 2.

The Intelligence of Animals

Human beings are supposed to be the smartest creatures on the planet. After all, we can solve problems. We can also use tools to help us work and play. But, are we the only animals that can do this? Scientists are learning a great deal about how other animals think and act. Some animals can solve problems and use tools.

Scientists know that dolphins are very intelligent. Dolphins can follow instructions and they have excellent memories. Dolphins can use tools, too. Scientists observed a pair of dolphins in a tank. The dolphins wanted to capture a moray eel partly hidden in a hole in some rocks. They worked as a team to catch their prey. One dolphin poked at the eel with the spine of the poisonous scorpion fish. The second dolphin waited at the other end of the hole. When the eel swam out to avoid the scorpion fish, it found a hungry dolphin. The dolphins showed that they could think and plan. They also showed that they could use another animal as a tool!

Scientists continue to study how animals solve problems and use tools. One day, we may understand more about the amazing animal mind.

Are Animals Inventors?

by Gail Jarrow and Paul Sherman

You use inventions every day. For some simple ones, think of a spoon or hammer. Other inventions are complex, such as a car or telephone. Many people think that only humans invent tools.

Not so fast. Some animals use tools, too. For example, fire ants use moss to soak up water and carry it home. Sea otters use rocks to crack open mussel shells. Does that mean that these animals are also inventors?

Finding out isn't easy. We can't ask an otter how it knew to use a rock as a hammer. Was it born knowing this? Or did it copy another otter's invention?

Scientists often approach these questions by watching animals in nature. They have noticed that all sea otters—young and old—use rocks to break hard shells. All do it basically the same way. And all fire ants use their moss the same way, too. So tool use by otters and fire ants may be an inborn ability.

The Termite Catcher

For some other animals, it's a different story. Chimpanzees use a stick to catch termites. A chimp finds a branch, strips off its leaves and side branches, and breaks the stick to the ideal length. Then it carefully pokes the tool into holes in a termite mound. The termites attack the stick. When the chimp pulls out the stick, it's covered with tasty termites. Unlike sea otters, individual chimps construct and handle their tools differently.

There is another clue that chimps invented this tool. Young chimps learn the skill by watching older chimps. The first few times a youngster makes a probe from a stick, the tool is crude and doesn't work well. By practicing, the young chimps improve their tool-making skill.

A Rodent's Dust Mask

Scientists gather more clues about an animal's use of tools by observing how the animal behaves in a new situation. Dr. Paul Sherman and Gabriela Shuster used this approach with naked mole-rats. These gerbil-sized African rodents live in underground tunnels, in colonies of up to three hundred members. In Dr. Sherman's laboratory at Cornell University, their homes are plastic tubes, in which they often gnaw holes with their large front teeth.

Before gnawing at the plastic, a mole-rat picks up a piece of wood shaving or root husk. The animal places the shaving or husk behind its front teeth. This shield keeps plastic dust out of the rodent's throat and windpipe while it gnaws.

Dr. Sherman and Ms. Shuster weren't sure when mole-rats started using these "dust masks." No one had noticed if the rodents used the wood shavings when the animals were first brought into the laboratories twenty years ago. Scientists also don't know if wild mole-rats use dust masks when they gnaw at dirt because no one has ever seen them working underground.

To learn more, Sherman and Shuster added bricks of fine sandstone, similar to the mole-rat's native soil, to the plastic tunnels. The mole-rats sometimes used the dust masks, but not as often as when they gnawed at plastic. When the researchers added cork, plastic foam, and clay, all of which broke off in chunks, the mole-rats never used wood shavings.

Did the mole-rats invent the dust mask to keep fine, irritating plastic out of their throats? Mole-rats in several laboratories use the wood shavings the same way. This could mean that naked mole-rats are born knowing how to shield their throats whenever digging creates fine dust.

But only the older mole-rats use the shavings. This could be a clue that the younger ones aren't born knowing how to use shavings as dust masks, but have to learn it from their elders. That would mean at least one mole-rat invented the tool. Instinct or invention? No one is sure yet.

A Puzzle for Ravens

Another animal tool-user is the raven. This bird collects rocks, then drops them on intruders. Is the raven inventive? To find out, Dr. Bernd Heinrich gave ravens a problem they had never seen before.

He tied meat to the end of a long string that was attached to a perch. The ravens could not pull bits of the meat loose by flying and grabbing at it. The only way to eat the meat was to pull the string up to the perch. But Dr. Heinrich made the problem harder by choosing a string that was too long to be raised with one pull.

At first the ravens pecked at the string or dived at the meat. Finally, one bird sat on the perch and pulled up a short length of string with its beak. The raven used its foot to clamp the string to the perch, which prevented the meat from falling back to its original place. The bird then used its beak to yank up another length of string. After repeating this several times, the bird could grab the meat.

Eventually, most of the other ravens pulled up the string in a similar way. Once a bird figured out the solution, it used the method perfectly every time. Because none of the ravens solved the problem immediately, Dr. Heinrich concluded that they had invented a solution.

Did some birds learn the solution by watching the first raven, or did each one figure out the problem alone? He couldn't tell, but his experiment showed that at least the first raven had been an inventor.

Animals other than humans probably won't invent complicated tools like computers or airplanes. But some of them are more inventive than you might think.

DIRECTIONS: Read each question carefully. Then write your answer in a paragraph on the lines.

1 In the first passage, you learned how dolphins used a tool to catch a moray eel. In the second passage, you learned how ravens pulled a string to get meat. Compare these two examples. Which do you think shows greater intelligence and why? Use details from the passages.

_____

_____

_____

_____

_____

_____

_____

Open the Door

This question asks you to compare and contrast information in two selections and evaluate meaning. The first thing you have to do is review the information in both selections. Think about how the dolphins solved their problem. Then think about how the ravens solved their problem. On a separate sheet of paper, write a few sentences summarizing each example. Then decide which example showed greater intelligence. Write a few sentences on the lines that explain your answer.

2   The second selection discusses how mole-rats use dust masks to keep tiny pieces of plastic out of their throats. The selection says scientists are unsure whether mole-rats learn how to make dust masks from other mole-rats or if they are born knowing how. What do you think? Give a reason for your answer.

_____

_____

_____

_____

_____

_____

_____

_____

Open the Door

Here you must extend the meaning of the selection and provide your own opinion. To answer this question, you need to go back to the second passage and reread the section about mole-rats and dust masks. What evidence in the passage supports the idea that mole-rats are born knowing how to use dust masks? What evidence supports the idea that mole-rats learn how to make the masks from other mole-rats? Which evidence is stronger? Why?

Speak Out

Imagine that you are a scientist researching the intelligence of animals. Prepare a speech about why you believe animals have the mind power to learn how to solve problems. Discuss several ways in which animals display their intelligence. Use information from both selections to prepare your speech. Then present it to the class.

Summary

In this unit, you have learned how to answer questions at three "key" levels of comprehension.

Find the Key

"Literal"

Look for information

Turn the Lock

"Interpretive"

Determine meaning

Open the Door

"Critical"

Go beyond the text

Remember that no matter what type of question you answer, you should always use the **Four *R*s: R**eady, **R**ead, **R**espond, **R**eview.

Ready—**Get ready to read**

► Set a purpose for reading
► Preview the selection
► Make predictions

Read—**Read the selection**

► Anticipate what will follow
► Monitor your understanding
► Confirm your predictions

Respond—**Answer the question**

► Read the question
► Think about it
► Answer the question

Review—**Check your answer**

UNIT 2

Graphic Organizers: The Key to Answering Essay Questions

The Essay Question

In Unit 1 you answered both multiple-choice and short-answer questions. Now you will learn how to answer essay questions, for which you will write responses of two or more paragraphs. Essay questions often require more thought and planning than other types of questions.

Get Organized!

You know how difficult it is to find something in a messy drawer. You search and search, but the item you are looking for escapes you in the clutter. However, finding something in a well-organized drawer is very easy. In the same way, you can answer an essay question more easily if you are organized before you begin to write.

A **graphic organizer** is a conceptual frame that allows you to collect ideas and categorize them. It helps you gather the information necessary to answer your essay question. Once you organize your ideas, it will be easier for you to write your essay.

In this unit, you will learn how to use different kinds of graphic organizers to answer essay questions. But first, here are some things to think about before you begin to write.

Before You Write

Before you write anything, ask yourself some questions:

1. *What is my topic?* What will you be writing about? State the topic in a few words. This will help you focus your writing.

2. *Why am I writing?* Think about the purpose of the essay. Usually you write to explain something, persuade someone, entertain someone, or describe something.

3. *Who will read my writing?* Consider who will be your audience. Your teacher will probably be your audience for a test.

This page may not be reproduced without permission of Steck-Vaughn/Berrent.

DIRECTIONS: Read this article about a new generation of cars that may replace the gas-powered automobile. Then you will use a Compare-Contrast Grid. It will help you compare and contrast gas-powered cars with electric cars.

The Cars of the Future

Americans spend a lot of time in their cars. Many people could not travel to work or shop for food without an automobile. Unfortunately, cars are a major source of pollution. When oil is in short supply, cars are also expensive to run.

Why doesn't a better type of car exist? In fact, it does. Electric cars have actually been around since 1888. Back then, electric cars were very popular. By 1912, there were 20,000 electric cars in use. More than 10,000 electric trucks and buses were on the streets. Even the President of the United States drove an electric car! People continued to drive electric cars until the 1940s.

Things changed after World War II. Americans felt strong and happy. They did not worry about wasting money. They did not care about polluting the air. They began driving cars with gas engines. In the 1960s and 1970s, people started to worry about

the environment. Oil became very expensive. Americans needed cars that were cheaper to run. Yet, the electric car still did not become popular. This is mainly because the car's battery needed to be recharged. Recharging the battery took three hours or more. That's a pretty long time to wait! Turning on the radio or the air conditioner drained the battery very quickly. Electric cars were also slower than gas-powered cars. They were heavier, too. People did not want to be bothered with electric cars.

In 1996 auto makers began improving the electric car. They built electric cars that were lighter and had fewer parts. These cars had batteries that could be recharged from an electrical outlet. These electric cars were better for people than gas-powered cars. They were cleaner and did not harm the air that people breathe. Still, few people bought these cars. Most people did not want to be bothered recharging the battery.

But the automobile industry is changing. People now realize that pollution is a serious problem. They know that it causes global warming. The hotter climate will cause many problems. The polar ice caps and glaciers will melt. Weather patterns will change. Diseases may spread more quickly in the heat. Auto makers are once again looking at the electric car.

A new type of electric car was created in 2000. It has both a gas tank and a battery. The gas tank is able to recharge the battery. This kind of vehicle is called a "hybrid." A hybrid is a combination of two different things. Because the cars have a gas tank, they do not need such large batteries. People may be willing to buy the cars now that they are lighter and faster. Soon, we should see more Americans driving electric cars. That will be a good change for the environment.

Compare-Contrast Grid

A **Compare-Contrast Grid** helps you compare and contrast certain features or characteristics of two things. Each *column* of the grid is labeled on the top with one of the subjects being compared. Each *row* of the grid is labeled on the left with a feature or characteristic being compared and contrasted.

Read the essay question and instructions on page 33.

FEATURE _____   _____

This page may not be reproduced without permission of Steck-Vaughn/Berrent.

Essay Question: Compare and contrast gas-powered cars with electric cars. You may discuss both the older and newer electric cars. Use facts and ideas from the article in your comparison.

1. You will be comparing and contrasting electric cars with gas-powered cars. At the top of the first column, write "Gas-Powered Cars." At the top of the second column, write "Electric-Powered Cars."

2. Next, write some features of the things you are comparing and contrasting. You might want to list features such as "pollution," "cost," "convenience of car," and "performance of car" in the feature column on the grid.

3. Fill in the grid as you read the story again. Write short phrases that tell about the features named in the grid. For some features, you may have to draw a conclusion based on what you read.

Now that you have filled in the **Compare-Contrast Grid,** use it to answer the essay question at the top of the page. Write your answer on a separate sheet of paper.

Turn the Lock

This question asks you to compare and contrast features of two types of cars by identifying details in the selection. To answer this interpretive question, think about what you learned in Unit 1. You must put together different pieces of information from the passage to form your response.

Look at the graphic organizer. Use the information you listed to write your essay. Write about how the cars are different first. Then, write about how the cars are the same.

Don't forget the fourth *R* in the **Four *R*s:** **R**eady, **R**ead, **R**espond, **Review**. It is now time to review your essay to make sure that your writing is the best it can be. To do this, use the checklist on page 56.

DIRECTIONS: Read this Native American story about a coyote that outwits himself. Then you will use a Character Traits Map. It will help you describe the coyote and the lesson he learns.

The Dust-Colored Coyote
A Pima Legend

adapted by Gay Seltzer

In the old days, when the world was new, Coyote was a pale green color. Vain and proud, he strutted through the Great Forest, sure that his fur was the loveliest in all creation. He sniffed grandly whenever he saw Owl or Beaver, sure that all he met were jealous of his beautiful green coat.

One day, as he was looking for something to eat, Coyote came to a clear, shimmering lake. Glancing at himself in the water, Coyote preened and pranced, posing this way and that to better admire his reflection.

"How grand I am," he said. "There is not another creature half as magnificent!"

Just then, at the far corner of the lake, Coyote saw an ugly little bird whose gray feathers sprouted from its skin at odd angles and in different shapes. The bird jumped into the clear water and began to sing.

Coyote laughed. "You are the silliest-looking bird I have ever seen!" he said. "You do not have one feather on your body that could be called lovely."

The bird did not pay a bit of attention but continued bathing in the shimmering water of the lake. Suddenly it fluttered from the lake and lay shivering on the bank. All of the ugly gray feathers floated to the earth until the bird lay quivering in its bare skin.

Coyote howled with laughter. The bird jumped into the lake once more. When it came out, it was covered with beautiful blue feathers. It hopped about and sang loudly, "This water is blue, and I am blue, too."

Coyote became very quiet. He looked once again at his reflection. Then he looked at the beautiful blue bird. Was Coyote still the finest-looking creature in the forest? He was no longer sure.

"I must have a blue coat like that," Coyote muttered to himself. "I absolutely must have a blue fur coat!"

Finally Coyote could stand it no longer. "Little blue bird," he cried, "you must tell me how you changed your ugly feathers to those beautiful blue ones! I will give you anything you want. But I must know your secret!"

The little bird fluttered his feathers to dry them. Then he began to smile. "I will gladly share my secret with you," he said. "But you must follow my directions carefully."

"I promise," said Coyote.

"This is a magic lake," said the bird. "Go into the lake four times in four days and sing the magic song. The fourth time, all your fur will fall off. Then, when you jump into the water a fifth time, all your fur will become this brilliant shade of blue."

"You must teach me the song," Coyote begged. "I must be that wonderful shade of blue!"

So the bird taught Coyote the song, and Coyote jumped into the lake four days in a row. The fourth time, all his fur fell off. After he jumped in the fifth time, his fur became a beautiful bright blue.

Well, was Coyote the proud one! He acted grander than ever. He believed he was more elegant than any other creature. He pranced and preened through the Great Forest, looking for Owl and Beaver to show them his brilliant blue fur.

Coyote found Beaver at the pond. "Look at me!" he called to his friend.

Beaver was busy. He dived again and again searching for food. All the while he ignored Coyote's calls.

"I said, 'Look at me'!" yelled Coyote once more.

Beaver was too busy.

Coyote lifted his head as high as he could, trying to catch Beaver's eye. "You are missing a wonderful sight!" he yelled.

Of course, with all this conversation, Coyote did not look where he was going. Suddenly he hit a tree stump and rolled over into the dust. He rolled and rolled. He could not get his balance. He rolled for so long that his breath was gone and clumps of his fur were stuck on bramblebushes and pine branches.

When Coyote finally got up, his beautiful blue fur was all dust colored! His once bushy tail was thin and straggly. And his pride had disappeared.

And that is why, ever since that day, all coyotes have been the color of dirt. And that is why, ever since that day, all coyotes hold their heads low and watch very carefully where they walk!

Character Traits Map

A **Character Traits Map** helps you organize your thoughts to gain insight into a character's personality traits. In this organizer, the name of the character goes in the center box. A character trait goes in each of the four triangular spaces coming off the center. Then, you follow each trait to the box labeled *Event*. In the box you write an event that illustrates the character trait.

Read the essay question and instructions on page 37.

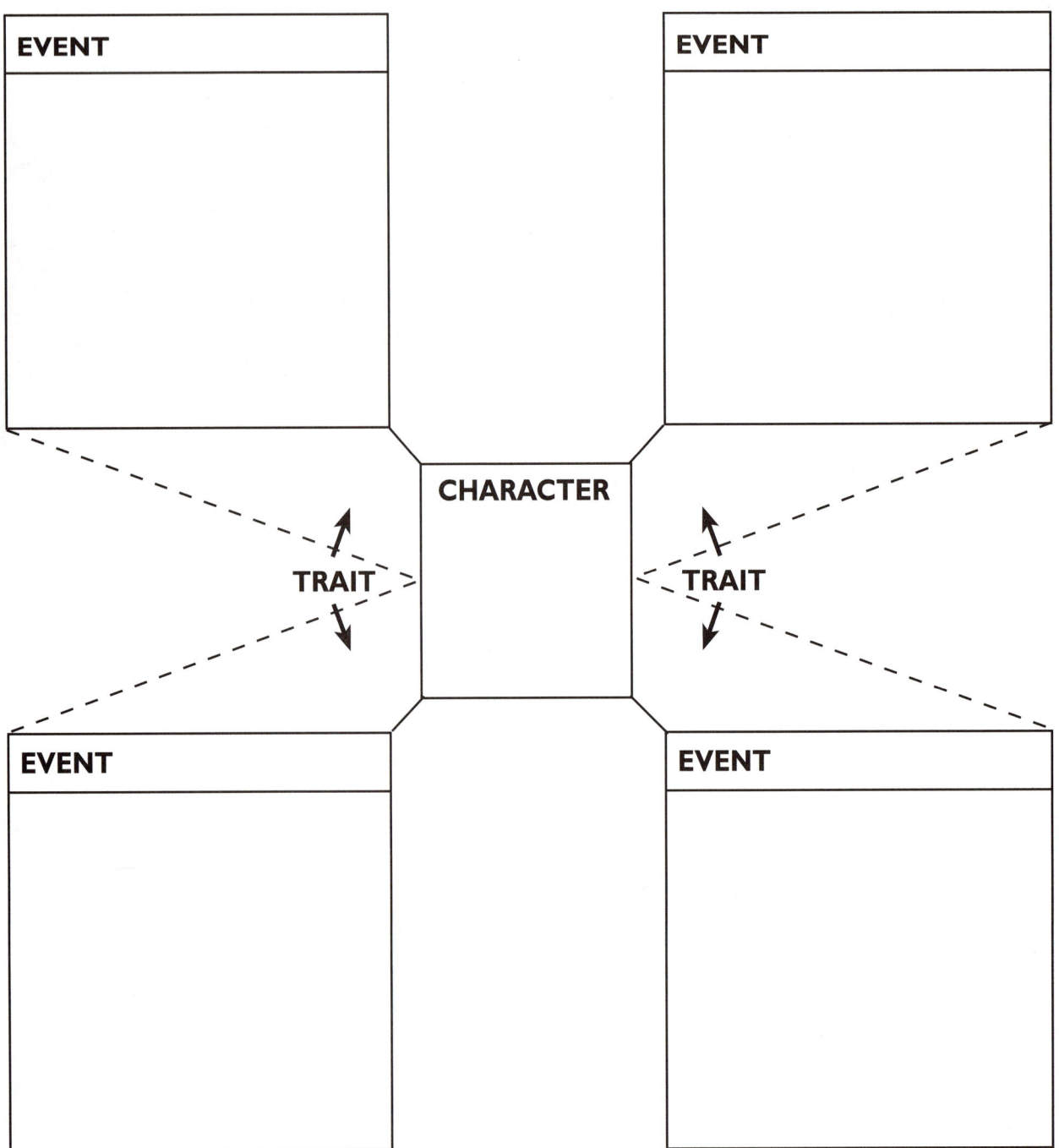

Essay Question: In the story, Coyote learns a valuable lesson. Why does he deserve to learn this lesson? Discuss Coyote's character traits and the lesson he needs to learn because of them.

1. The question asks you to identify some character traits that made Coyote deserve the lesson he learns. Since Coyote is the character you will be writing about, write his name in the center box of the graphic organizer.

2. Next, think about different character traits that Coyote possesses. A character trait is a word that describes Coyote's personality. To determine Coyote's character traits, look back at the things that he says, thinks, and does. Write a character trait in each of the four spaces.

3. Now follow each of Coyote's traits up or down to its "Event" box. Go back to the story to find an event that illustrates the character trait. Then write this event in the box.

Now that you have filled in the **Character Traits Map,** use it to answer the essay question at the top of the page. Write your answer on a separate sheet of paper.

Open the Door

This question asks you to analyze a character by determining his character traits. To answer this critical question, you must go beyond the text and make a judgment about what you have read.

Look at the graphic organizer you just filled in. Write about each trait you listed. Explain how you identified these traits through Coyote's words, thoughts, and actions. To help with your explanation, look at the event you listed for each trait. Then state the lesson Coyote learned and how he learned it.

Don't forget the fourth **R** in the **Four R**s: **R**eady, **R**ead, **R**espond, **R**eview. It is now time to review your answer. Make sure that your writing is the best it can be. To do this, use the checklist on page 56.

Speak Out

Now that you have read this legend about Coyote, think about how the Pima people must have viewed this animal. Do you think Coyote was admired or made fun of? Why? Give a short speech to a group of classmates about Coyote's role in the animal kingdom.

DIRECTIONS: Read the following two selections about a special area of Arizona. Then you will use a Flow Chart. It will help you plan an imaginary vacation here.

The History of Navajo County

Navajo County was first formed on March 21, 1895. It is the fourth largest county in Arizona. The county is located on high plateaus on the banks of the Little Colorado River. The borders of Navajo County run north through the Navajo and Hopi reservations. They extend south to the White Mountains, the Apache Reservation, and the Mongollon Rim.

The landscape of the Navajo County is varied. In the north, there are rugged, dry deserts. This area is called plateau country. Huge mesas rise up from the ground. In between these mesas are deep canyons. In some of these canyons are ancient cliff-dwellings such as those at Canyon de Chelly. Long ago, people lived in these dwellings. In the south, the land is heavily wooded with ponderosa pine, piñon, and juniper.

Over a half of Navajo County is Indian reservation land. The historical trading post of Kayenta, founded in 1909, is now the gateway to the Navajo Tribal Park at Monument Valley. The Hopi Reservation is south of this park. It includes the Hopi Pueblo of Oraibi. Oraibi is one of the oldest settlements in the United States. Tribal people have lived there for hundreds of years.

Each year, thousands of people visit Navajo County. Some come to see the beautiful views and enjoy the warm weather. Others come to learn about Native American culture. Most reservations allow tourists to see their ceremonial dances and other tribal events. Local artists sell paintings, crafts, and jewelry. Campers enjoy visiting Navajo County's many parks.

CAMPING IN Navajo County Parks

**Our parks have beautiful campgrounds
that are perfect for families—like yours!**

Cholla Lake Park has a public camping ground near Petrified Forest National Park. It also contains Cholla Lake, where you can enjoy boating and swimming. Campsites have running water, RV hookups, and other conveniences. A park ranger will help you plan your visit to Cholla Lake Park. Stop by or call to make reservations for your camping trip. We're located in Holbrook, one mile off I-40, Exit 277.

Show Low Lake is a cool spot even on the hottest summer days. High in the White Mountains, Show Low Lake offers campers wooded forests and a lake where the fish are always jumping! Older campers receive a special discount. Shop at our camp store and check out boat rentals at our friendly Visitor's Center. We're right off State Route 260.

Tall Timbers Heber/Overgaard Park lies among the ponderosa pines of the Apache Sitgreaves National Forest. Come for a day or stay overnight. Play racquetball, softball, volleyball, horseshoes, and shuffleboard. We also have an archery range and a children's playground. You can find us just south of Overgaard on State Route 260.

The Recreation Center offers great picnic spots and a children's playground. Enjoy three lighted racquetball courts or join a volleyball game. You'll find us two miles south of Holbrook on State Route 77.

Little Painted Desert has some spectacular desert views! Come and see 660 acres of colorful rock formations. This is a wonderful place for a picnic! We're just off Exit 257, near the Navajo National Indian Reservation.

Flow Chart

A **Flow Chart** helps you put information in a logical order. This is a good way to organize explanations and instructions. In this organizer, the purpose of your plan goes in the heading at the top. Then you use the boxes for the steps in your explanation. You can adjust the number of boxes to fit the steps in your plan.

Read the essay question and instructions on page 41.

Purpose: _____

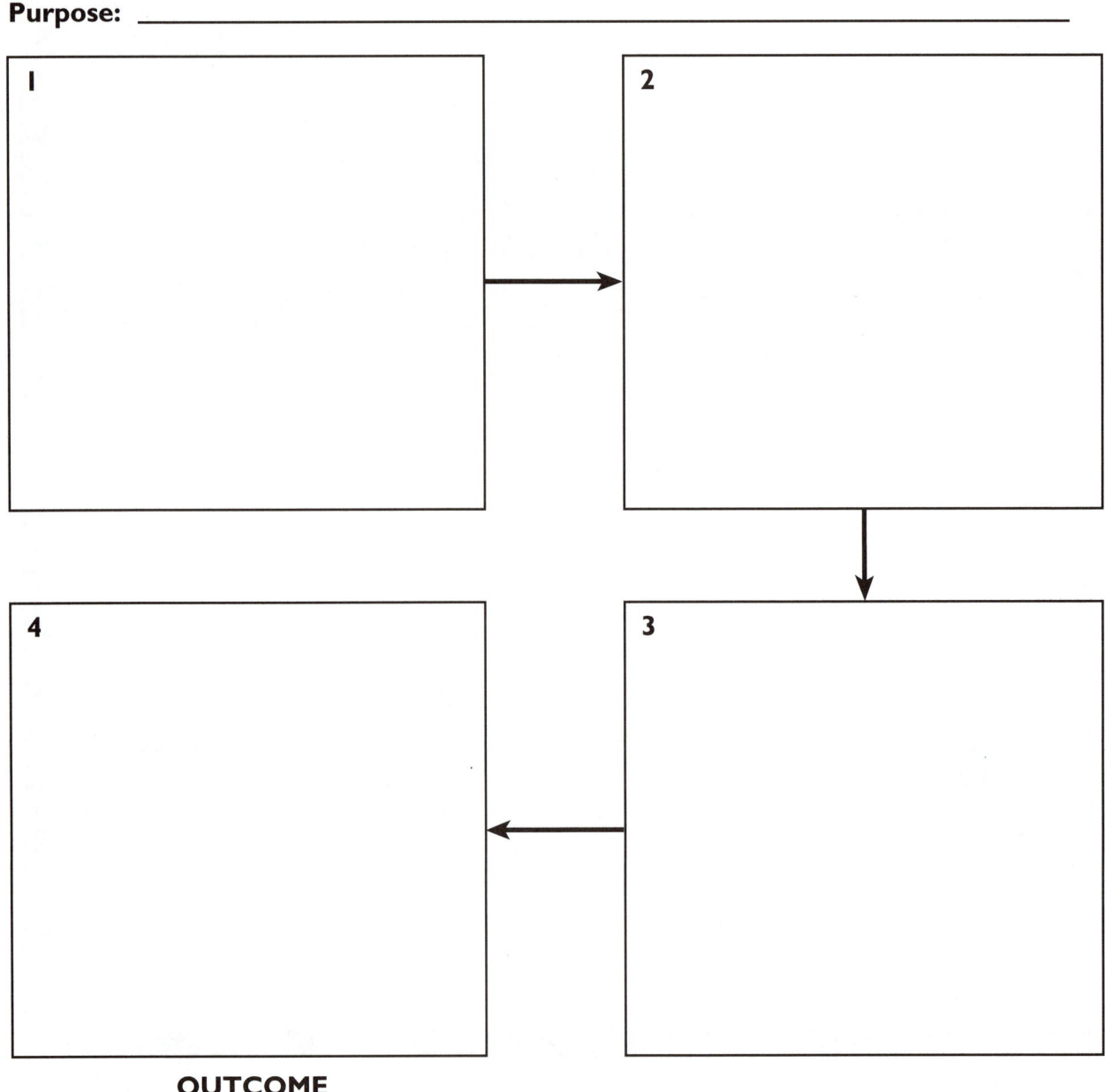

OUTCOME

Essay Question: Imagine that you are planning a vacation in Navajo County, Arizona. Which places would you choose to visit? Why? What would you do in each place? Describe your itinerary, or plans, for a week in Navajo County.

1. First, think about your purpose, or what you plan to do. State this purpose at the top of the organizer, on the line provided.

2. Next, you have to figure out the steps of your plan. Where do you want to go? What will you do there? Use the two selections to help you decide. You will write the steps in order in the boxes on your flow chart.

3. Finally, use the last box in your organizer to write a comment or two about the outcome of your plan. That will be helpful when you write a short conclusion to your essay.

Now that you have filled in the **Flow Chart,** use it to answer the essay question at the top of the page. Write your answer on a separate sheet of paper.

Open the Door

This question asks you to evaluate and extend the meaning of the information in the selections. To answer this critical question, think about what you learned in Unit 1. You must take the information you have learned from the selections and go beyond the text by using your judgment.

Use the information in the two selections to answer the essay question. Think about what you might like to do on your vacation. Which places in Navajo County would you most like to explore? What would you do on each day of your trip? How long do you plan to stay in each place? Use details from the selections in your essay.

Remember to **Review**. Use the checklist on page 56 to review your work.

DIRECTIONS: Read the following poem about a magical experience. Then you will use an Overall Impression Map. It will help you describe the poem's impression on you.

The Bean-Stalk

by Edna St. Vincent Millay

Ho, Giant! This is I!
I have built me a bean-stalk into your sky!
La,—but it's lovely, up so high!

This is how I came,—I put
Here my knee, there my foot,
Up and up, from shoot to shoot—
And the blessèd bean-stalk thinning
Like the mischief all the time,
Till it took me rocking, spinning,
In a dizzy, sunny circle,
Making angles with the root,
Far and out above the **cackle**
Of the city I was born in,
Till the little dirty city
In the light so sheer and sunny
Shone as dazzling bright and pretty
As the money that you find
In a dream of finding money—
What a wind! What a morning!—

cackle: *noise*

Till the tiny, shiny city,

When I shot a glance below,

Shaken with a **giddy** laughter,

Sick and blissfully afraid,

Was a dew-drop on a blade,

And a pair of moments after

Was the whirling guess I made,—

And the wind was like a whip

Cracking past my icy ears,

And my hair stood out behind,

And my eyes were full of tears,

Wide-open and cold,

More tears than they could hold,

The wind was blowing so,

And my teeth were in a row,

Dry and grinning,

And I felt my foot slip,

And I scratched the wind and whined,

And I clutched the stalk and **jabbered,**

With my eyes shut blind,—

What a wind! What a wind!

giddy: dizzy or unsteady

jabbered: spoke quickly and without sense

Overall Impression Map

An **Overall Impression Map** helps you keep track of the details you find and observations you make as you read. These details and observations add up to an overall impression of the story. In this organizer, fill in the outside bubbles with the appropriate information about touch, sound, sight, and other details. Then, draw some conclusions about how these details add up by making a statement about the overall impression in the center bubble.

Read the essay question and instructions on page 45.

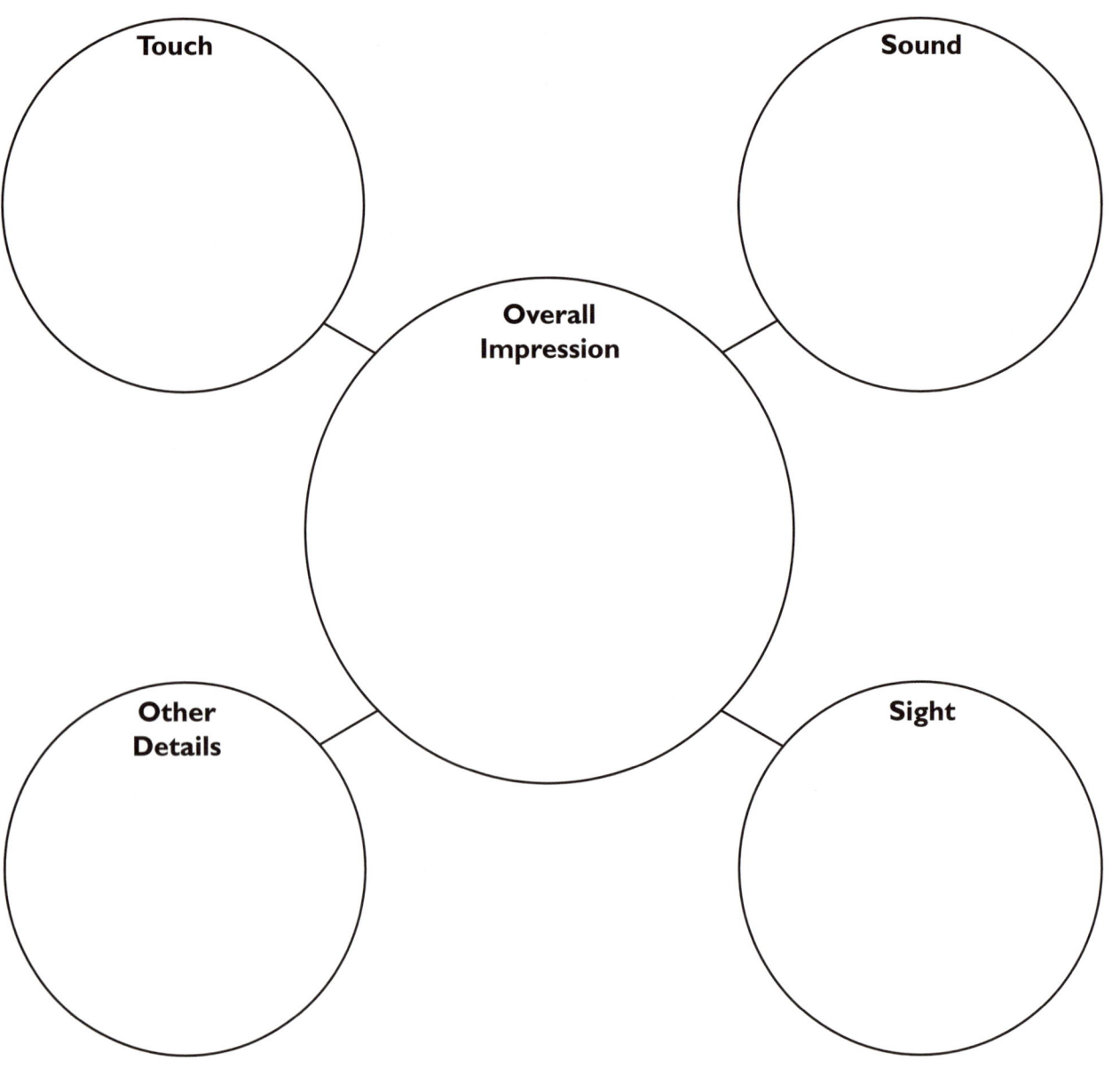

Essay Question: What is the poem's total impression, or impact, on you? Describe how the sensory details of the poem contribute to your overall impression.

1. Record details relating to what the speaker of the poem hears, sees, and touches in each of the labeled bubbles of the organizer. You will notice that the poet uses many sensory details to create a feeling of excitement in the poem.

2. Use the bubble labeled "Other Details" to record details that do not seem to fit in any of the other bubbles. What other kinds of observations did you make while reading this poem?

3. Finally, write a sentence or two that sums up your overall impression in the center bubble of the map.

Now that you have filled in the **Overall Impression Map,** use it to answer the essay question at the top of the page. Write your answer on a separate sheet of paper.

Open the Door

This question asks you to describe your impression of the poem. To answer this critical question, you must go beyond the text and make a judgment about what you have read.

Look at the graphic organizer you just filled in. Then think about what effect the poem has on you. How does it make you feel? How do the details in the poem listed in the organizer contribute to this effect?

Remember to **Review**. Check your writing on page 56.

DIRECTIONS: **Read this article about the famous story of Peter Pan and the author J. M. Barrie. Then you will use a Facts and Opinions Map. It will help you explain why J. M. Barrie wrote this story.**

Who Was Peter Pan?

by Kristina Cliff-Evans

Peter Pan was an imaginary boy who decided not to grow up and went to Neverland to live forever with the Lost Boys. Everyone knows that, right?

Yes, but did you know that for its author, Sir James Matthew Barrie, *Peter Pan* was the fulfillment of a promise? Long before he wrote the famous tale, before he became very rich and was given the title of **baronet,** he made a secret promise in his heart to his mother.

Sir J. M. Barrie was born in a Scottish village called Kirriemuir in the county of Angus. The year was 1860, and he was born on May 9 at number nine Brechin Road. This house, like most buildings in Kirriemuir, gave off a faint pink glow in the sunset because of its red sandstone structure. The town was famous for the nearby quarry that colored its buildings. James loved Kirriemuir and learned its nickname, "The Little Red Town," from his mother, Margaret, who had lived there all her life.

A portrait of J. M. Barrie

Generations of Kirriemuir families made their livings at handloom weaving. David Barrie, James's father, was no exception. The tiny family home had only four rooms and was full of children—James was the ninth of ten in the family and lived there until he was eight years old. The Barries had beds everywhere, even in the kitchen. The main room of their home was taken up completely by the large, wooden loom at which Mr. Barrie worked, weaving sturdy damask cloth. The spare threads that always dangled from its sides came to be known as thrums—a word James liked so much that he often used Thrums as the name of the hometown in his stories.

Little James looked up to his big brother, David, but when James was six, a terrible thing happened. On the night before David was to turn fourteen, he died in a skating accident. James was very sad, but his mother was crushed. In her heartbreak, she became distant from her other children and could not seem to accept David's death.

baronet: a British title similar to a baron

James watched his mother's grief and longed to help her feel better. He was much smaller than David, but he wanted to make up for his brother's loss. He thought his mother would be happy again if she could always have a young son. In his child's way of understanding, he decided that he would not grow up at all but would stay a child for his mother—forever.

James loved to make up stories and plays. The family's wash house sat across from their cottage on the other side of narrow Brechin Road. For his mother it served to do the laundry for her big family. For James it was an ideal theater. He had a built-in cast of characters in his family and friends, and the little one-room building saw his stories come to life.

Soon, of course, he realized that he couldn't stay a little boy and fulfill his secret promise. His mother loved all of her children, but she never completely recovered from losing her oldest boy. By the time James was a teenager, he saw that, while he would grow up and leave home, David would be thirteen forever. His mother already had a son who would never grow up, David.

J. M. Barrie would write for more than fifty years. His work includes seventeen novels and other stories, thirty-nine plays, and over five hundred articles published in magazines and journals. His plays were popular in Britain and the United States. He had no children of his own but spent a great deal of time with the five sons of a close friend. They often acted out the stories that Barrie dreamed up. In 1902, he wrote a novel called "The Little White Bird" using ideas from his play with the boys. Peter Pan was a character in the story.

A Statue of Peter Pan stands in Kensington Gardens in London England.

It was in 1904, however, that James introduced the boy who would never grow up to the world. *Peter Pan* was a huge hit. It not only made James famous but earned him half a million pounds in only two years. King George V personally honored James in 1913 by making him a baronet.

If writing *Peter Pan* made a fortune for James, it is the great fortune of children all over the world to visit Neverland with Peter and Wendy through reading. For a short time, every child lives that lovely fantasy of never growing old.

Who was Peter Pan? He was the little boy inside James Matthew Barrie who longed to give his mother everlasting joy. And he is surely that true child in every person who never completely grows up.

Facts and Opinions Map

A *fact* can be proven or checked. An *opinion* states what a person believes or feels is true. Unlike facts, opinions cannot be proven. A **Facts and Opinions Map** helps you distinguish and organize facts and opinions from the article. In this organizer, you list the facts from the article, as well as supporting details, in the box labeled "Facts." You list the opinions stated in the article, as well as supporting details, in the box labeled "Opinions."

Read the essay question and instructions on page 49.

FACTS	OPINIONS

Essay Question: According to the author of the article, why did J. M. Barrie write *Peter Pan*? Use facts and opinions from the article in your summary.

1. First, look for facts about why J. M. Barrie wrote *Peter Pan*. Remember, facts can be proved. You would prove a fact by doing further research or using personal observation. Write each fact you find in the box that is marked "Facts." Each time you record a fact stated in the article, write down any additional details the author gives about this piece of information.

2. Then, look for statements of opinion about why Barrie wrote *Peter Pan*. Remember, an opinion expresses a feeling or belief and cannot be checked. Use the box marked "Opinions" to note these ideas. Each time you record an opinion expressed in the article, write down any supporting details the author includes to back up her opinion.

Now that you have filled in the **Facts and Opinions Map,** use it to answer the essay question at the top of the page. Write your answer on a separate sheet of paper.

Open the Door

This question asks you to identify facts and opinions in the article, in order to summarize the main idea. To answer this critical question, make a judgment about what you have read.

You can use the information from the organizer to answer the essay question. To write your essay, consider both the information presented and how the author feels about what she is writing. What facts support her ideas? What opinions does she express in the selection? In your essay, be sure to separate the facts of the story from the author's opinions and from your own opinions.

4Rs Remember to **Review**. When you are finished, check your writing on page 56.

DIRECTIONS: Read this excerpt from a novel about climbers in the Swiss Alps. Then you will use an Event Map. It will help you write a summary of the story.

A Boy and a Man

from *Banner in the Sky*

by James Ramsey Ullman

It is 1865. Sixteen-year-old Rudi loves to climb in the Alps of his native Switzerland. He dreams of scaling the peak of the Matterhorn, something that has never before been done. But on this day, something even more important is at stake—a man's life.

The crevasse was about six feet wide at the top and narrowed gradually as it went down. But how deep it was Rudi could not tell. After a few feet the blue walls of ice curved away at a sharp slant, and what was below the curve was hidden from sight.

"Hello!" Rudi called.

"Hello—" A voice answered from the depths.

"How far down are you?"

"I'm not sure. About twenty feet, I'd guess."

"On the bottom?"

"No. I can't even see the bottom. I was lucky and hit a ledge."

The voice spoke in German, but with a strange accent. Whoever was down there, Rudi knew, it was not one of the men of the valley.

"Are you hurt?" he called.

"Nothing broken—no," said the voice. "Just shaken up some. And cold."

"How long have you been there?"

"About three hours."

Rudi looked up and down the crevasse. He was thinking desperately of what he could do.

"Do you have a rope?" asked the voice.

"No."

"How many of you are there?"

"Only me."

There was a silence. When the voice spoke again, it was still quiet and under strict control. "Then you'll have to get help," it said.

Rudi didn't answer. To get down to Kurtal would take at least two hours, and for a party to climb back up would take three. By that time it would be night, and the man would have been in the crevasse for eight hours. He would be frozen to death.

"No," said Rudi, "it would take too long."

"What else is there to do?"

Rudi's eyes moved over the ice walls: almost vertical, smooth as glass. "Have you an ax?" he asked.

"No. I lost it when I fell. It dropped to the bottom."

"Have you tried to climb?"

"Yes. But I can't get a hold."

There was another silence. Rudi's lips tightened, and when he spoke again his voice was strained. "I'll think of something," he cried. "I'll think of *something*!"

"Don't lose your head," the voice said. "The only way is to go down for help."

"But you'll—

"Maybe. And maybe not. That's a chance we'll have to take."

The voice was as quiet as ever. And, hearing it, Rudi was suddenly ashamed. Here was he, safe on the glacier's surface, showing fear and despair, while the one below, facing almost certain death, remained calm and controlled. Whoever it was down there, it was a real man. A brave man.

Rudi drew in a long, slow breath. With his climbing-staff he felt down along the smooth surface of the ice walls.

"Are you still there?" said the voice.

"Yes," he said.

"You had better go."

"Wait—

Lying flat on the glacier, he leaned over the rim of the crevasse and lowered the staff as far as it would go. Its end came almost to the curve in the walls.

"Can you see it?" he asked.

"See what?" said the man.

Obviously he couldn't. Standing up, Rudi removed his jacket and tied it by one sleeve to the curved end of the staff. Then, holding the other end, he again lay prone and lowered his staff and jacket.

"Can you see it now?" he asked.

"Yes," said the man.

"How far above you is it?"

"About ten feet."

Again the staff came up. Rudi took off his shirt and tied one of its sleeves to the dangling sleeve of the jacket. This time, as he lay down, the ice bit, cold and rough, into his bare chest; but he scarcely noticed it. With his arms extended, all the shirt and half the jacket were out of sight beneath the curve in the crevasse.

"How near are you now?" he called.

"Not far," said the voice.

"Can you reach it?"

"I'm trying."

There was the sound of scraping boot-nails; of labored breathing. But no pull on the shirtsleeve down below.

"I can't make it," said the voice. It was fainter than before.

"Wait," said Rudi.

For the third time he raised the staff. He took off his trousers. He tied a trouser-leg to the loose sleeve of the shirt. Then he pulled, one by one, at all the knots he had made: between staff and jacket, jacket and shirt, shirt and trousers. He pulled until the blood pounded in his head and the knots were as tight as his strength could make them. This done, he stepped back from the crevasse to the point where his toes had rested when he lay flat. With feet and hands he kicked and scraped the ice until he had made two holes. Then, lying down as before, he dug his toes deep into them. He was naked now, except for his shoes, stockings and underpants. The cold rose from the ice into his blood and bones. He lowered the staff and knotted clothes like a sort of crazy fishing line.

The trousers, the shirt and half of the jacket passed out of sight. He was leaning over as far as he could.

"Can you reach it now?" he called.

"Yes," the voice answered.

"All right. Come on."

"You won't be able to hold me. I'll pull you in."

"No, you won't."

He braced himself. The pull came. His toes went taut in their ice-holds and his hands tightened on the staff until the knuckles showed white. Again he heard a scraping sound below, and he knew that the man was clawing his boots against the ice-wall, trying both to lever himself up and to take as much weight as possible off the improvised lifeline. But the wall obviously offered little help. Almost all his weight was on the lifeline. Suddenly there was a jerk, as one of the knots in the clothing slipped, and the staff was almost wrenched from Rudi's hands. But the knot held. And his hands held. He tried to call down, "All right?" but he had no breath for words. From below, the only sound was the scraping of boots on ice.

How long it went on Rudi could never have said. Perhaps only for a minute or so. But it seemed like hours. And then at last—at last—it happened. A hand came into view around the curve of the crevasse wall: a hand gripping the twisted fabric of his jacket, and than a second hand rising slowly above it. A head appeared. A pair of shoulders. A face was raised for an instant and then lowered. Again one hand moved slowly up past the other.

But Rudi no longer saw it, for now his eyes were shut tight with the strain. His teeth were clamped, the cords of his neck bulged, the muscles of his arm felt as if he were being drawn one by one from the bones that held them. He began to lose his toeholds. He was being dragged forward. Desperately, frantically, he dug in with his feet, pressed his whole body down, as if he could make it part of the glacier. Though all but naked on the ice, he was pouring with sweat. Somehow he stopped the slipping. Somehow he held on. But now suddenly the strain was even worse, for the man had reached the lower end of the staff. The slight "give" of the stretched clothing was gone, and in its place was rigid deadweight on a length of wood. The climber was close now. But heavy. Indescribably heavy. Rudi's hands ached and burned, as if it were a rod of hot lead that they clung to. It was not a mere man he was holding, but a giant; or a block of granite. The pull was unendurable. The pain unendurable. He could hold on no longer. His hands were opening. It was all over.

And then it was over. The weight was gone. There was a scraping sound close beneath him; a hand on the rim of ice; a figure pulling itself up onto the lip of the crevasse. The man was beside Rudi, turning to him, staring at him.

"Why—you're just a boy!" he said in astonishment.

Event Map

An **Event Map** helps you organize your thoughts by asking key questions, similar to those of a newspaper reporter. In this organizer, a question appears in each box. These questions ask the following: What? When? Where? Who? How? Why? Write each answer in the appropriate box.

Read the essay question and instructions on page 55.

What happened?

When did it happen?

Where did it happen?

Who was involved?

How did it happen?

Why did it happen?

Essay Question: Imagine that you are a reporter for a newspaper in the town where Rudi lives. Write an article describing the events that happen in the story.

1. The graphic organizer will help you gather the information you need to write your news article. Look at the question in the first box. What was the main event that happened in the story? Write it in the first box.

2. In the next two boxes, write when and where the event happened.

3. In the third box, write the names or descriptions of the characters involved. In the fourth box, give details on how the event unfolded.

4. In the last box, tell why the event happened. Why did Rudi do what he did?

Now that you have filled in the **Event Map,** use it to answer the essay question at the top of the page. Write your answer on a separate sheet of paper.

Turn the Lock

This question asks you to summarize what you have read about by identifying details from the article. To answer this interpretive question, think about what you learned in Unit 1. You must put together different pieces of information from the passage to form your response.

Look at the answers you wrote for each question on the graphic organizer. Think about how you would use these answers to write your article. Remember that you are writing the article from the viewpoint of a reporter who has learned about the exciting rescue of the trapped climber. Think about how newspaper articles are organized. Try to mimic this organization when you write your article.

Remember to **Review**. Use the checklist on page 56 to review your work.

After You Write

Use this list to check your writing.

Revise:

☐ Did you meet the purpose of the task?

☐ Did you stay on the topic?

☐ Is there an opening and a closing?

☐ Did you support your main ideas?

☐ Did you organize your ideas clearly?

☐ Did you vary your words and sentences?

☐ Do all the words make sense?

☐ Is your writing interesting?

☐ Is your writing easy to read?

Edit:

☐ Do verbs agree with their subjects?

☐ Are pronouns used correctly?

☐ Are the spelling, capitalization, and punctuation correct?

Summary

In this unit, you learned that you can use graphic organizers to help you recall and understand what you have read. Graphic organizers can also help you answer essay questions about a passage by allowing you to collect ideas and categorize them before you begin to write.

You have learned about the following graphic organizers:

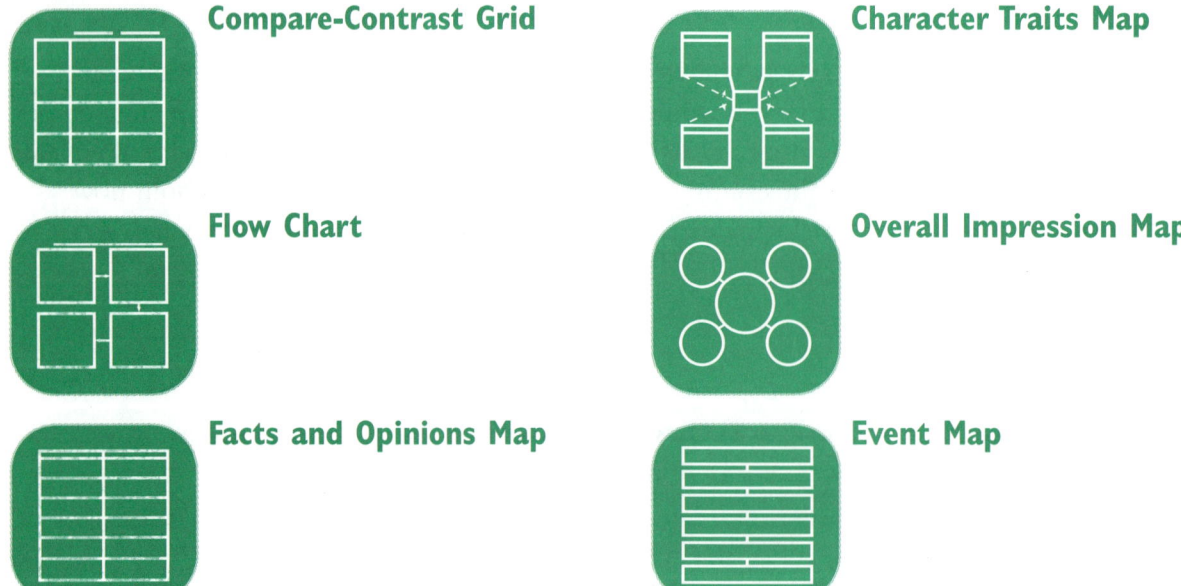

Compare-Contrast Grid

Character Traits Map

Flow Chart

Overall Impression Map

Facts and Opinions Map

Event Map

4Rs

Remember that when answering an essay question, you should always use the **Four *R*s:** **R**eady, **R**ead, **R**espond, **R**eview. When you review your work, use a checklist such as the one above.

UNIT 3

Guided Practice

Now you are going to practice what you have learned by reading several selections and answering multiple-choice, short-answer, and essay questions about them. These questions will be at the three key levels of comprehension: literal, interpretive, and critical. You will be given a hint to help you answer each question.

Regardless of what type of selection you read or question you answer, you should always follow the **Four *R*s:**

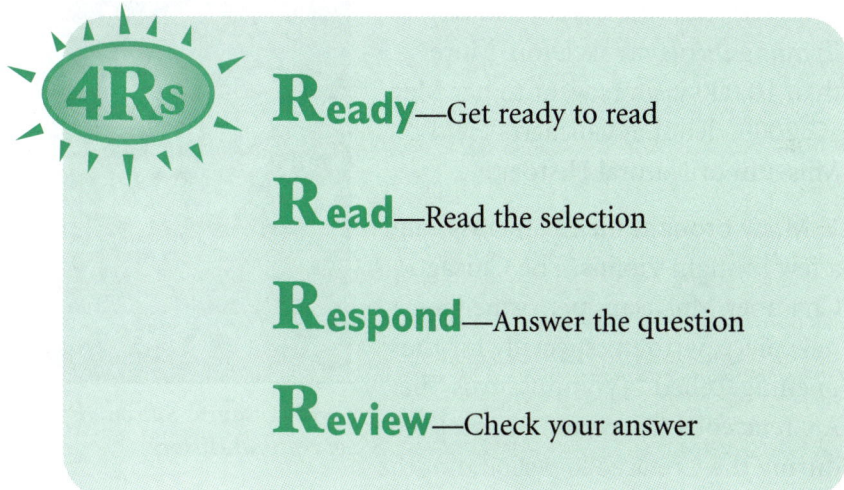

4Rs

Ready—Get ready to read

Read—Read the selection

Respond—Answer the question

Review—Check your answer

DIRECTIONS: Read this article about an exciting scientific discovery. Then answer questions 1 through 6. Darken the circle at the bottom of the page or write your answer on the lines.

Tyrannosaurus Sue

The Prehistoric Giant Stands Again

Sue is a sensation. It's not just that she's 42 feet long and 65 million years old. She's the world's most complete, best preserved, and largest *Tyrannosaurus rex* skeleton. More than 10,000 visitors went to her May 17, 2000, debut at Chicago's Field Museum of Natural History.

Many brought their cameras—and a few brought violins. The Chicago Chamber Musicians performed a new piece, written especially for the opening, called "Tyrannosaurus Sue: A Cretaceous Concerto." (*T. rex* lived during the Cretaceous period, not the Jurassic period, as many believe.)

Tyrannosaurus Sue on display at Chicago's Field Museum of Natural History

Rest in Pieces

Amazingly, more than 200 of Sue's bones were preserved. The skeleton includes the most complete *T. rex* tail ever found, as well as one of only two *T. rex* arms ever found. Sue's skull contains the longest (and scariest) *T. rex* tooth yet known—it's a foot long.

One amazing discovery in Sue's skeleton is that she has a wishbone, or furcula, such as you would find in most bird skeletons. This is the first wishbone found on a *T. rex*. It supports the theory that birds evolved from dinosaurs, either directly or from a common ancestor.

Even though Sue's bones are more than 65 million years old, they are so well preserved that you can see marks where muscles and tendons once lay.

Slow, But Deadly

Studies of Sue's foot bones have indicated that *T. rex* probably walked at about 6 mph and ran at not more than 15 mph, much slower than previously thought.

The lead researcher on Sue says that the way the *T. rex* moved in the movie *Jurassic Park* was probably very accurate. Most likely *T. rex* bent over so that its huge tail did not touch the ground, and walked on its toes—*T. rex* is *digitigrade*, meaning it walks on its toes like a cat. (People are *plantigrade*, meaning we walk flat-footed.)

But the movie was wrong in suggesting that *T. rex* would have to see its prey move in order to find it—from studying Sue, researchers have determined that *T. rex* had an excellent sense of smell. Sue's skull reveals that in a *T. rex* the olfactory nodes were much larger than the cerebrum.

Sue or Sir?

Tyrannosaurus Sue was named for Sue Hendrickson, the fossil hunter who found the skeleton in 1990. But although the skeleton is generally referred to as a "she," no one really knows whether Tyrannosaurus Sue was male or female. The skeleton's very large size could suggest that the dinosaur was female, because among birds of prey—*T. rex's* closest ancestors—females are generally larger than males.

Senior Sue

Throughout her life Sue suffered some hard knocks, including broken ribs and an injured arm. Although scientists do not know exactly what illnesses dinosaurs had, it looks as though Sue was affected by an age-related disease much like arthritis. "Here is a very, very old dinosaur that just got sick and died after a long, active life," says John Flynn, a Field Museum paleontologist.

Just how old was she? Scientists don't know for sure how long a *T. rex* might have lived. Says Flynn, "We know turtles and crocodiles can live to 150 years, and they are cold-blooded. We know some birds, which are warm-blooded, can live for many decades. My guess is that dinosaurs could live for decades, some 100 years or more."

Queen of the Dinosaurs

For many of the researchers who have gotten to know Sue, the discovery of the massive *T. rex* was the event of a lifetime. "It's truly a dream fossil," says Tony Wentz, who worked to dig Sue out of the ground and helped prepare her skeleton for the exhibit. "It's the best of the best, the biggest, the most well-preserved. Everything you could ever want in digging a dinosaur was in Sue."

1 Scientists believe that Tyrannosaurus Sue was very old because—

   A she was the largest *T. rex* ever discovered

   B she had many bumps and bruises

   C she may have had an age-related disease

   D she had traveled very far

   Hint Identify details from the article. Scan the article to find the place where the author discusses Sue's age. Why do scientists think she lived a long life?

2 Why did the author state in the article that more than 10,000 visitors went to see Tyrannosaurus Sue on the first day of the exhibit?

   F He wanted to make a point of how popular Sue is.

   G He wanted to show how well-known Chicago's Field Museum of Natural History is.

   H He wanted to explain why some people brought their violins.

   J He wanted to support his previous statement of how well preserved Sue is.

   Hint Determine the author's purpose. Look for where the author mentions the visitors. Read the sentences before and after this statement. What message is the author trying to send?

3 Which of the following is an *opinion* from the article?

   A More than 200 of Sue's bones were preserved.

   B This is the first wishbone found on a *T. rex*.

   C Everything you could ever want in digging a dinosaur was in Sue.

   D Turtles and crocodiles can live to 150 years, and they are cold-blooded.

   Hint Remember that a *fact* can be proved. An *opinion* is someone's belief. Which statement sounds like someone's belief?

Answers

1 Ⓐ Ⓑ © Ⓓ	**2** Ⓕ Ⓖ Ⓗ Ⓙ	**3** Ⓐ Ⓑ © Ⓓ

4 Why do scientists believe that birds evolved from dinosaurs?

_____

_____

_____

_____

_____

_____

 **Hint** Identify details. Scan the article to find the place where the author discusses birds of prey. What do dinosaurs and birds have in common?

5 What makes Tyrannosaurus Sue different from other *T. rex* skeletons?

_____

_____

_____

_____

_____

_____

Hint Determine the main idea. Look back at the article to see why scientists were so excited about Sue. What makes this *T. rex* so special?

6 Imagine that you are a scientist presenting Tyrannosaurus Sue as your new discovery to a group of experts. Write a summary of the most important findings about the special *T. rex.* Include both facts and opinions from the article in your summary.

Use a graphic organizer to plan your summary.

 Draw a Facts and Opinions Map to organize information from the article. List the facts in one column and theories and opinions in the other column. Think about how you will introduce your topic.

Write your summary on the lines below. If you need more space, continue writing on a separate sheet of paper.

_____

_____

_____

_____

_____

_____

_____

_____

_____

_____

_____

_____

_____

_____

_____

_____

 **Hint** Summarize what you have read by identifying details from the article. Use the information on the Facts and Opinions Map to write your summary. Include those facts and details that are most important, as well as theories that have arisen. Be sure to organize your information clearly and logically. Remember to use the checklist on page 56 to review your writing.

DIRECTIONS: Read this story about two very different sisters and a school talent contest. Then answer questions 7 through 12. Darken the circle at the bottom of the page or write your answer on the lines.

The Talent Show

Nandi Harrison was a girl who could get things done. That is what her teachers, her parents, and her friends always said. So it was no surprise when Nandi was chosen to organize the school's talent contest.

Nandi was thrilled, that is until her little sister, Val, insisted on entering the competition.

"I'm going to do my gymnastics routine!" Val announced cheerfully, digging into her pancakes with such enthusiasm that she knocked over the bottle of maple syrup.

"What?" Nandi put down her fork and frowned.

"Nandi, eat your breakfast," her mother replied mildly.

"But Mom—can't you see we have a problem here?" She could picture the disaster so clearly. Everything would be going smoothly until her clumsy little sister embarrassed her with the worst gymnastics performance ever seen at Hopewell Elementary School. It was Nandi's last year at Hopewell, and she wanted to end her school career on a note of triumph.

"We'll discuss it after dinner," Mrs. Harrison said firmly. "I have to be at work by nine o' clock sharp."

Val danced away from the table, her dress already splotched with maple syrup. In the hallway, she turned a cartwheel and fell into the end table, nearly knocking over the lamp.

"Not in the house," Mrs. Harrison *reproved* her. "You can cartwheel on the lawn."

Nandi sighed heavily and shook her head at her sister's back.

At school, there was a lot of excited talk about the contest. Howard Weiser promised to do magic tricks. Caitlin Reilly would perform a dance solo. And more students were signing up every hour.

During lunch, Val trotted up to Nandi. "My teacher says I'll be the star of the show!" she said and giggled. Then she dashed off to her table to finish lunch with some of her second-grade friends.

Nandi tried to erase the frown from her face. Surely Mom would make Val understand that she just wasn't good enough to perform on stage. Val could do her stunts in gymnastics class where nobody really cared how awkwardly she back-flipped and somersaulted.

After dinner, Nandi caught her mother in the kitchen.

"Yes, honey?" asked Mrs. Harrison, her hands in soapy water.

"I'll dry the dishes." Nandi grabbed a towel. As she worked, she peered out of the kitchen window. Val was attempting a handstand against the trunk of the elm tree.

"About this talent contest—you have to stop Val from entering it!"

"Is there an age limit on contestants?" her mother asked.

"No," Nandi admitted. "But there should be a requirement about the amount of talent a participant has."

Mom shrugged. "You know, Nandi, it's just a school event. It won't be on television." She turned off the faucets and leaned against the counter. "There she goes again," Mom said as Val landed hard on the ground.

"Lucky we had a lot of rain this month," Nandi said. "At least the grass is soft when she falls."

Her mother laughed.

Val didn't think the competition was anything to laugh about. She practiced every day.

"I'm getting really good at my back flips," she declared. "And you should see my cartwheels!"

"I've seen them," Nandi answered. But that's all she said. Mom would not stop Val from performing. So Nandi had to include her name in the program. Disaster!

Finally, there were only three days until the show. Nandi had the program printed and organized a bake sale. Everything was under control. There was only one wild card, and that was her own little sister. When the show began, Nandi stood backstage with her clipboard, giving instructions to the entrants. Everything was going as planned. The audience applauded each act, and Nandi kept the show on track.

Then it was time for the younger children to perform. Out trotted two tap dancers, who made it through their act without a hitch. They bowed and ran back to the wings.

Nandi winced when she had to announce her own sister's name. Out came Val, wearing a huge grin. She began with a series of back flips. Nandi groaned softly when Val's back hit the floor with a thud. But Val picked herself up and did the flip again, this time completing it properly. She leaped across the stage and somersaulted onto a mat. Then she threw herself into a series of cartwheels. One, two, three, perfect cartwheels! The audience cheered.

When Val danced back stage, Nandi caught her sister in a warm hug. "I never believed you could do it," she admitted.

"Well, of course I could," Val laughed. "All I needed was a little practice."

7 Nandi does not want Val to enter the talent contest because—

   F she is afraid Val will embarrass her

   G she thinks gymnastics is silly

   H she is worried that Val will get hurt

   J she hopes that she will win it herself

 Hint Identify details. Reread the part of the story where Val first says she is planning to enter the talent contest. How does Nandi feel? Why does she feel this way?

8 What does the word *reproved* mean?

   A replied

   B scolded

   C suggested

   D praised

 **Hint** This is a vocabulary question. Think about Val's actions. How does Mrs. Harrison feel about what Val is doing?

9 Which word *best* describes Val?

   F troublesome

   G determined

   H spoiled

   J humorous

 Hint Determine character traits. Think about what Val says and does in this story. How does she feel about the talent contest?

Answers

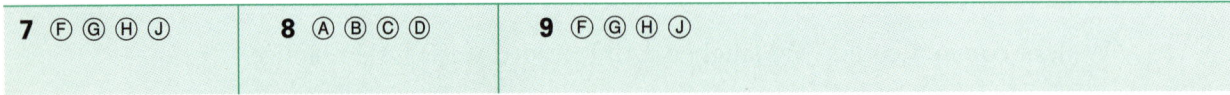

7 Ⓕ Ⓖ Ⓗ Ⓙ	**8** Ⓐ Ⓑ Ⓒ Ⓓ	**9** Ⓕ Ⓖ Ⓗ Ⓙ

10 Why does Mrs. Harrison let Val enter the talent contest?

_____

_____

_____

_____

_____

_____

Hint Determine meaning in the story. What does Mrs. Harrison tell Nandi about the talent show? What does this suggest about her attitude toward this school event?

11 What lesson does Nandi learn at the end of the story?

_____

_____

_____

_____

_____

_____

Hint Evaluate meaning. What does Nandi say and do after Val's gymnastics routine? How does she seem to feel about what her sister has achieved?

12   A character sketch is a description of a character in a story. It includes details and examples to show what he or she is like. Write a character sketch for Nandi. Use details from the story to support your answer.

Use a graphic organizer to plan your character sketch.

 Draw a Character Traits Map. Reread the story and use the graphic organizer to record observations about Nandi. Write Nandi's character traits in the four triangular spaces coming off the center of the graphic organizer. In each event box, write an event in which this character trait is displayed.

Write your character sketch on the lines below. If you need more space, continue writing on a separate sheet of paper.

_____

_____

_____

_____

_____

_____

_____

_____

_____

_____

_____

_____

_____

_____

_____

_____

Hint Determine character traits by identifying details from the story. Use the information in the Character Traits Map to write Nandi's character sketch. Identify Nandi's character traits. Include events from the story that show Nandi displaying these traits.

DIRECTIONS: Read this article about a famous magician of the twentieth century. Then answer questions 13 through 18. Darken the circle at the bottom of the page or write your answer on the lines.

Harry Houdini: The Great Escape Artist

Harry Houdini was the best-known magician of his time. His magic tricks were amazing, and he was a sensational performer. He was born in Hungary in 1874 as Eric Weiss. However, Houdini spent most of his life in America. Assisted by his wife Bessie, Houdini entertained audiences with incredible tricks and **feats.** He became known for amazing escapes. Houdini could get out of all sorts of locks, handcuffs, straightjackets, ropes, and sealed containers. Houdini also had a special style that was all his own.

Ropes and Knots

Luckily for students of magic, Houdini shared his secrets. In 1912 he published a book titled *Magical Rope Ties and Escapes.* The author knew all about ropes and knots. He had also figured out a way to be tied that would allow him to escape quickly. Houdini explained what he did when he was tied with a sixty-foot rope. He gave away an important fact: you cannot tie someone securely in a standing position with a knot at either end of the body. If the rope is simply wound around the body, the performer can wriggle out of it. Sometimes however, the person doing the tying is wise to the trick. In that case, that person will make many knots in the rope. The more knots made, the harder it will be to escape. Houdini told readers what to do then:

". . . swell the muscles, expand the chest, slightly hunch the shoulders, and hold the arm a little way from the sides. After a little practice you will find that such artifices will enable you to **balk** the most knowing ones . . ."

Houdini was strong and flexible. This helped him get out of tightly tied knots. Fans were amazed to see him make his way out of the rope. They didn't know his secret: he hid a sharp, hooked knife in his clothing. If the knots were too difficult, he cut off a short piece of the rope's end.

Handcuff Tricks

Houdini was also known for his handcuff tricks. Many other magicians did stunts

feats: deeds or acts of accomplishment
balk: fool

with handcuffs. Houdini was the best, however. Early in his career, he was called the "Handcuff King." He carefully studied the design of locks. He collected them so that he would remember how each kind closed and opened. He found that he could open some kinds of handcuffs without keys. For others, though, he had to hide a key somewhere close by. Then, he would use his hands, teeth, or a special rod to handle the key. He had incredible skill. In his 1910 book *Handcuff Secrets*, Houdini told how old-fashioned handcuffs could be opened with a shoestring. He made a loop in the string. Then he lassoed the end of the screw in the locks and pulled the bolt back. Other cuffs could be opened with a sharp knock against a hard object. Sometimes, Houdini wore a lead plate around his knee, under his pants, for this purpose. He also used trick cuffs that were not actually locked.

The Milk Can

Houdini also perfected a trick called the milk can escape. Before he performed it, he would bang on the can to prove to the audience that it was sturdy. Assistants filled the large container with twenty pails of water. Houdini wore a bathing suit to perform the trick. He scared audiences with a description of the trick. He told them what it was like to hold his breath and risk drowning. He explained what it was like to be trapped in a tight space. His helper Kukol stood by with an ax. Kukol was ready to smash the milk can if Houdini did not come out on time.

Houdini left an explanation of his famous milk can escape. Parts of the container were not firmly joined and could be separated. Soon Houdini would pop out, smiling calmly at his fans. No one would be able to tell that the container had been tampered with in any way.

A True Performer

Houdini carefully scripted his performances. What he said on stage was almost as important as what he did. His style kept his career alive even when movies became popular. In the past, many people enjoyed watching magicians. Then along came film. All sorts of exciting illusions could be projected onto a movie screen. Magicians struggled to keep up with the thrilling pace of movies. Houdini's acts became more and more dramatic.

Houdini became an actor to gain a wider audience. He developed stunts that could be performed outdoors. He began to make escapes while dangling from the new skyscrapers in the big cities. He did his container tricks in rivers. This added a new element of danger.

Houdini performed many kinds of tricks. However, he is best remembered as a master escape artist. Many entertainers copied his tricks, but few had his acting ability. As he wrote in his book *Handcuff Secrets*, "You will notice that some of these tricks are very simple—but remember it is not the trick that is to be considered, but the style and manner in which it is presented."

13 How did Houdini escape from tight knots in ropes?

    A He untied the knots in the ropes.

    B He cut the ropes with a knife.

    C He pulled the ropes apart.

    D He stood tall and kept his back straight.

 **Hint** Identify details. Reread the section about Houdini's rope tricks. What did he do if the knots were tied tightly?

14 From the selection you can conclude that Houdini shared his secrets—

    F to make a great deal of money

    G to teach other magicians his tricks

    H to get more people to attend his shows

    J to prove that he was better than other magicians

 **Hint** Draw a conclusion. Reread the quotes from Houdini's books and read the words before and after them. What was he mainly trying to do?

15 To learn more about Harry Houdini, you should—

    A read a biography about him

    B look in an encyclopedia under "Magic"

    C visit the cities where Houdini performed

    D look up *Houdini* in the dictionary

 **Hint** Determine characteristics of informational text. Think about which source would provide the most information about the topic. This is the correct choice.

Answers

13 Ⓐ Ⓑ Ⓒ Ⓓ	**14** Ⓕ Ⓖ Ⓗ Ⓙ	**15** Ⓐ Ⓑ Ⓒ Ⓓ

16 Why did Houdini become an actor?

_____

_____

_____

_____

_____

_____

Hint Identify details in the selection. Reread the end of the article. What happened that made magicians less popular?

17 Why was Houdini called the "Handcuff King"?

_____

_____

_____

_____

_____

_____

Hint Identify details. Reread the section "Handcuff Tricks." Why did people call him the "Handcuff King"?

18   Imagine that you are the great Harry Houdini. Choose one of the tricks described in the article and write a short speech for your audience. You will be giving this speech as you do the trick.

Use a graphic organizer to plan your speech.

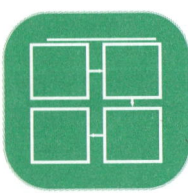 Draw a Flow Chart. Fill in each box on the chart with what you will say for each step needed to perform the trick. Be sure to organize the steps so that they represent a beginning, middle, and end.

Write your speech on the lines below. If you need more space, continue writing on a separate sheet of paper.

_____

_____

_____

_____

_____

_____

_____

_____

_____

_____

_____

_____

 **Hint** Extend the meaning of the article by summarizing information and the sequence of events. Use the information from your Flow Chart to write your essay. Remember to include details about the trick that you found in the article. Consider how Houdini might have acted when he performed the trick. Use the checklist on page 56 to review your work.

 *Speak Out*

Now give your speech to the class.

DIRECTIONS: Read this poem about a person's memories, then answer questions 19 through 24. Darken the circle at the bottom of the page or write your answer on the lines.

Long Ago

by Eugene Field

I once knew all the birds that came

    And nested in our orchard trees,

For every flower I had a name—

    My friends were woodchucks, toads, and bees;

I knew where **thrived in yonder glen**

    What plants would soothe a stone-bruised toe—

Oh, I was very **learned** then,

    But that was very long ago.

I knew the spot upon the hill

    Where checkerberries could be found,

I knew the rushes near the mill

    Where pickerel lay that weighed a pound!

I knew the wood—the very tree

    Where lived the **poaching, saucy crow,**

And all the woods and crows knew me—

    But that was very long ago.

thrived in yonder glen: lived and grew in a nearby valley
learned: educated
poaching, saucy crow: a crow that steals and is rude

And pining for the joys of youth,

    I tread the old familiar spot

Only to learn a solemn truth;

    I have forgotten, am forgot.

Yet here's this youngster at my knee

    Knows all the things I used to know;

To think I once was wise as he!—

    But that was very long ago.

I know it's folly to complain

    Of whatsoe'er the fates decree,

Yet, were not wishes all in vain,

    I tell you what my wish should be:

I'd wish to be a boy again,

    Back with the friends I used to know,

For I was, oh, so happy then—

    But that was very long ago!

▸ **Of whatsoe'er the fates decree:** of whatever shall happen

19 Read these lines from the poem.

> **I knew the wood—the very tree**
>
> **Where lived the poaching, saucy crow,**

The phrase "poaching, saucy crow" is an example of—

F a metaphor

G personification

H imagery

J a simile

 Hint Imagery involves description of a mental picture. Personification gives human qualities to something that is not human. Both a metaphor and a simile compare things, but a simile uses *like* or *as*.

20 How does the speaker feel when he recalls his childhood self?

A curious

B regretful

C joyful

D anxious

 **Hint** Determine the mood of the poem. Think about what the speaker says about his childhood days. What age would the speaker like to be?

21 Why does the speaker say that the youngster is wiser than he?

F The youngster knows things about the natural world that the speaker has forgotten.

G The youngster does not wish for impossible things, unlike the speaker.

H The speaker realizes he has wasted his childhood.

J The youngster teaches the speaker about animals and plants.

 Hint Draw a conclusion. Look at the third stanza of the poem.

Answers

19 Ⓕ Ⓖ Ⓗ Ⓙ	20 Ⓐ Ⓑ Ⓒ Ⓓ	21 Ⓕ Ⓖ Ⓗ Ⓙ

22   What friends did the speaker have in his childhood days?

_____

_____

_____

_____

_____

_____

Hint   Identify details. Look at the first two stanzas of the poem.

23   What is the main idea of the poem?

_____

_____

_____

_____

_____

_____

Hint   Determine the main idea. What is the poem mostly about?

24 In the poem, the writer discusses a place he has known well since childhood. Write a description of this place based on the details in the poem. Where do you think this place could be? What would you find there? Describe the scene well enough so that a visitor could recognize it easily.

Use a graphic organizer to plan your description.

 Draw an Overall Impression Map. Use it to organize the details in your description. Each outside bubble should contain one or more details relating to sound, sight, touch, and any other details. In the center bubble, draw some conclusions about how these details add up to an overall impression.

Write your description on the lines below. If you need more space, continue writing on a separate sheet of paper.

_____

_____

_____

_____

_____

_____

_____

_____

_____

_____

_____

_____

_____

_____

_____

 Hint This question asks you to summarize the poem and the effect it has on you. Use the information from your Overall Impression Map to write your description. Tell what kinds of plants and animals you would find in this place, and describe the natural setting in which they live. Use the checklist on page 56 to review your writing.

DIRECTIONS: Read these two stories from different countries. The first comes from ancient Japan. The second is a Greek myth that was first told thousands of years ago. Then answer questions 25 through 30. Darken the circle at the bottom of the page or write your answer on the lines.

Amaterasu, the Sun Goddess

adapted by Matt Evans

This story comes from Japan. Amaterasu is the supreme goddess of the Shinto religion, and is much loved and revered throughout the country.

One day, a very long time ago, Izanami, the mother of all, and Izanagi, the father of all, gave birth to a beautiful little girl. She was bright and radiant and her light filled the land.

She was so dazzling that her mother exclaimed, "Our daughter is the most wondrous of all our children. We must not keep her on Earth. Let us place her high in Heaven, that she may rule the sky."

The young girl was truly beautiful, and she climbed high into the sky where she could look down on the lands below.

To the plants and animals, she provided warmth and light. She taught the people how to weave cloth, and how to grow rice and **millet**. All loved her dearly and named her Amaterasu Omikami, which meant Heaven Shining Great Woman.

Amaterasu had a younger brother who was very loud and frightening. His name was Susanowo, which meant Brave Strong Impetuous Man. He ruled the mighty oceans.

Susanowo wasn't like his sister. He was angry and loud, and stomped across the earth, tearing whole mountains up and making great valleys with his feet. Even his breath tore the branches off of the trees.

One day their father, Izanagi, called to Susanowo and said, "My son, I gave you the seas to rule and instead you tear across the land. You are too dangerous for the Earth. You have caused much damage and have frightened many people. Since you cannot control your temper I must ask you to leave."

Susanowo was furious. He stomped away extra hard, traveling across the land and straight up into Heaven.

Amaterasu greeted her brother, and after hearing of his exile from the world below,

millet: a cereal grain

offered to let him live in Heaven with her.

Susanowo promised his sister that he would be better behaved and thanked her deeply for her hospitality.

It was not very long until Susanowo's behavior returned to normal. Soon he was tearing up the lands of Heaven just as he had below.

First he chased his sister's precious horses.

Then he tore down Heaven's rice fields and smashed the irrigation ditches, ruining the season's harvest.

He wrecked many buildings and smashed the beautiful mountains that Amaterasu loved to view from her home.

Finally she could take it no more and fled.

She ran to a large cave, ducked inside, and pulled a huge boulder down to block the entrance.

Suddenly the sun was gone. Darkness closed over the lands of Heaven and Earth and everyone cried out, "Amaterasu, come back!"

But as much as they cried and pleaded, the boulder never moved and Amaterasu never answered.

Hundreds of gods and goddesses gathered outside the cave to discuss how they might persuade Amaterasu to come out.

Soon the God of Wisdom, Omohi Kane, came up with a plan and shared it with everyone.

They gathered many roosters and placed them outside the cave entrance. Then they planted a large tree with hundreds of branches and decorated it with bright cloth and banners.

Next they made a ring of fire to drive away the darkness.

Lastly, the round-cheeked fun-loving Goddess of Mirth, Ama-no-uzume, stood atop an overturned barrel and danced a comical dance that set the crowd laughing.

Inside the cave Amaterasu heard the crowing of the roosters and scratched her head. Then she heard the laughter of the people gathered outside the cave.

She was puzzled and called out "How is it that everyone is laughing when it is so dark outside?"

Ama-no-uzume called back, "Because out here there is a goddess who is just as bright as you!"

Amaterasu grew so curious that she opened the door a tiny crack to see what was going on and looked right into a large mirror that had been placed near the cave.

She saw that there was another who was just as bright as she, and stared in wonder at her own dazzling reflection.

Just then Tajikarawo, the God of Strong Hands, gently took hold of Amaterasu's arm and drew her out into the festivities.

With Amaterasu out of the cave, daylight returned to the world and all the gods and goddesses cheered. The sky was blue again, the animals and people were no longer cold, and the crops began to grow once more.

They continued with their grand party and danced away for many hours to celebrate.

Demeter and Persephone

Demeter was the goddess of the harvest. She kept the earth fruitful so that flowers could bloom and crops could grow. Demeter had a lovely daughter named Persephone. One day, Persephone was picking flowers with her friends. Suddenly, the earth opened up and Hades, the god of the underworld, emerged. He carried Persephone away with him to the underworld, where the souls of the dead lived.

When Demeter learned what had happened, she wept many tears. She swore that the earth would give no more crops until her daughter came back to her. The world became a terrible place. Nothing would grow, and people went hungry. The people cried out for help, but Demeter would not change her mind.

Finally, Zeus, the ruler of the gods grew worried. He told Hermes, the messenger of the gods, to go down to the underworld and rescue Persephone. However, this was a difficult task, because Persephone was not allowed to leave. Hades said that once a person had eaten the food of the underworld, he or she could not return to the earth. Persephone had eaten one pomegranate seed, so she had to stay in the underworld. Hades wanted Persephone to be his queen.

Zeus sent his mother, Rhea, down to reason with Hades. Rhea persuaded Hades to let Persephone be with her mother for part of each year. The girl would spend the winter in the underworld, but each spring she would return to the earth.

Mother and daughter were grateful for the chance to be together again. Demeter let the flowers and crops grow. Each spring, Persephone graced the earth with warmth and beauty. Seeds grew into flowers and fruits. The fields of grain began to grow again. The earth welcomed Persephone, and the birds sang sweetly. But when autumn days became chill and gray, Persephone knew it was time for her to return to the kingdom of the dead. Then the world grew once again dark and cold.

25 Why does Izanagi send his son, Susanowo, away from the earth?

   A Susanowo has a very bad temper.

   B Izanagi wants him to rule the sky.

   C Susanowo wants to be with his sister in Heaven.

   D Izanagi hopes he can help his sister out of a cave.

 Hint Identify details from the first story. Reread the part of the story that discusses Susanowo. What does he do that gets him into trouble?

26 Hades would not let Persephone return to the earth because—

   F he was angry with Demeter, her mother

   G she had eaten some food in the underworld

   H he wanted flowers and fruits to grow in the underworld

   J she had promised to be his queen

 Hint This is a cause-and-effect question. Identify the reason why Hades will not let Persephone return to earth. Scan the story to find the part where Hades says Persephone must stay in the underworld. What has Persephone done?

27 Amaterasu, the sun goddess, and Persephone, Demeter's daughter, symbolize—

   A hunger

   B winter

   C power

   D life

 Hint Make a connection between the two stories. A symbol in literature is a person, object, or event that stands for an idea or a set of ideas. What do Amaterasu and Persephone stand for?

Answers

25 Ⓐ Ⓑ Ⓒ Ⓓ	**26** Ⓕ Ⓖ Ⓗ Ⓙ	**27** Ⓐ Ⓑ Ⓒ Ⓓ

28 What happens when Persephone returns to the earth each year?

_____

_____

_____

_____

_____

_____

_____

Hint Summarize the information. Reread the end of the second story. How does the earth change when Persephone returns?

29 How did Ama-no-uzume trick Amaterasu to come out of the cave?

_____

_____

_____

_____

_____

_____

_____

Hint Summarize the information. Look the end of the first story. What does Ama-no-uzume do?

30   Compare the two myths. What is their common theme? In what ways are they alike and different?

Use a graphic organizer to plan your essay.

Draw a Compare-Contrast Grid. Then use it to compare and contrast the two stories. In the first column, focus on the features such as theme, relationships, setting, nature elements, and realism of story. In the next two columns, elaborate with details from each myth.

Write your essay on the lines below. If you need more space, continue writing on a separate sheet of paper.

_____

_____

_____

_____

_____

_____

_____

_____

_____

_____

_____

_____

 **Hint** Make connections between the two myths by comparing and contrasting, as well as determining theme. Use the information from your Compare-Contrast Grid to organize your essay. Discuss the theme, or message, of each tale and support your interpretation with details from the two selections. Use the information about each feature that you wrote in the organizer. Remember to use the checklist on page 56 to review your writing.

Test

You will now be taking a practice test that includes all the skills you have reviewed in this book. Follow the directions in each section. As always, remember to use the **Four *R*s: R**eady, **R**ead, **R**espond, and **R**eview. You may look back at the reading passages as needed.

For the multiple-choice questions, work carefully and try to get as many questions right as you can. Do not spend too much time on any one question. If you are not sure of an answer, make the best choice you can and go on to the next question. You can go back and check answers later if you have time.

For the open-ended questions, plan out what you want to say before writing. Use graphic organizers to help you write your essays. Make sure that you respond to all parts of each item. After you finish writing, use the checklist on page 56 to help you review your work.

DIRECTIONS: Read this article about a legendary king who may have lived hundreds of years ago. Then answer questions 1 through 11. Darken the circle on the separate answer sheet or write your answer on the lines.

King Arthur: Truth or Tale

Do you enjoy reading old legends and stories of distant days? Perhaps the most famous legend of all is that of King Arthur. The story of Arthur, King of Britain, is full of romance and magic. Historians have spent a lot of time researching the story of Arthur to see if it is history or just a story.

The Legend of King Arthur

It is said that Arthur was the son of Uther Pendragon, an English king who lived during the sixth century. Young Arthur was raised as an ordinary child by a foster-father, Sir Ector. Arthur had no idea that he was of royal blood.

Then one day, when it was time to choose a new king, a great tournament was held. Arthur went in search of a sword for the knight he served. He came upon a great stone that held an **anvil.** A sword was stuck in the anvil. Arthur pulled it out with ease and brought it to the tournament. All the nobles were amazed because that sword was the famous *Excalibur*. Only the true king of all Britain could pull *Excalibur* out of the stone. Merlin, the court magician, informed the crowd that this simple boy was really the son of King Uther Pendragon. And so young Arthur took over the throne.

King Arthur became a wise and powerful ruler. He founded the Knights of the Round Table at Camelot. Only the best and bravest men could hold a seat at the king's council table. Some of the most famous of these were Sir Lancelot, Sir Gawain, Sir Percival, and Sir Tristram. The knights often left Camelot to go in search of adventure.

anvil: a large iron block

They fought for their king, defending the weak and punishing the *unjust.* They rescued fair ladies and performed other great deeds. In time, Arthur married Guinevere, the most beautiful woman in the kingdom.

All was not well in Camelot, though. Arthur's sister was a **sorceress,** named Morgan Le Fay. She and her son, Sir Mordred, became Arthur's sworn enemies. In the end, Mordred wounded Arthur in battle. It is said that Arthur did not die but was carried off to Avalon. The legends say that one day Arthur will return.

Were the Characters Real?

The story of Arthur and his court has many elements of a fairy tale. Wizards, witches, and enchanted swords are certainly not the stuff of history. Yet, several historians wrote about a great king named Arthur. Geoffrey of Monmouth tells that Arthur's grandfather, Conan Meriadoc, came from Brittany and founded the English dynasty. That would have taken place in the fifth century. A later historian, Geoffrey Ashe, says that the real King Arthur was Riothamus, a king of Brittany. His army might have crossed the English Channel to fight the Visigoths in the year 468. This king fled to England during the civil wars in Brittany but returned to his native land to drive out the Germanic invaders. If this man was the King Arthur of the legends, he would have lived fifty years earlier than Geoffrey of Monmouth claims.

Was Arthur's queen, Guinevere, a real person? This has not been proven. In the various Arthur stories, she is always beautiful but not always faithful to her king. Some say she fell in love with Sir Lancelot. Others say she also helped Mordred kill King Arthur. In some versions of the story, she is tricked into behaving wrongfully and is forgiven for what she does.

The stories also disagree on how Guinevere died. She was either killed by Lancelot, died peacefully in a convent, or met her end as a prisoner of Mordred's evil followers. Geoffrey of Monmouth wrote that Guinevere was the daughter of a Roman nobleman. Malory, a fifteenth-century English writer, is the author of a famous series of Arthurian stories. Malory referred to Guinevere as the daughter of King Leodegrance. She has also been described as a German princess and as the offspring of King Ogrfan Gawr, a mighty giant of Wales. Some say that when the monks of Glastonbury discovered Arthur's grave in 1191, Guinevere's bones were not buried with those of her husband. In fact, little is known about Arthur's queen. However, she is certainly a major character in Arthurian legend.

There is also the mysterious magician named Merlin to consider. He was a wizard who served as young Arthur's tutor, secretly preparing the boy for the kingship. In the stories, Merlin helped Arthur break the spell and gain *Excalibur.* He also helped create the Round Table and used his powers to guide events at Camelot. When Arthur was wounded, Merlin went with him to the Isle of Avalon to be healed.

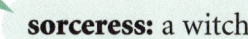

sorceress: a witch

Could a magician such as Merlin actually have existed? Once again, we must hear from Geoffrey of Monmouth. Geoffrey wrote that Merlin, or Myrddin, was a sixth-century prophet from the north of Britain. He may have been the son of a royal princess. There were many rumors about Merlin. Some said that his father was an evil spirit. Although this is hard to believe, there was a good deal of mystery surrounding Merlin's parents. But even if his parents were bad, Merlin certainly used his own powers to do good. And even if there was no such person as this wizard, he is one of the most important figures in these tales.

Arthur Lives On

How should we view the Arthurian legends? Are they history or simply wonderful stories? There are probably some seeds of truth in the tales. A powerful Briton king once ruled the land. He would have had many followers. Maybe he was guided by a wise man such as Merlin. It is easy to imagine that a great king would find a lovely wife. In time, many additional stories were told about the doings of this king and his court. After many years, Arthur became a symbol of wise rule and high adventure. People would not let his story die. So they declared that he was not really gone, but resting. That is why Arthur was last seen at Avalon, one day to return to England.

1 You can tell from the article that *unjust* means—

A lost

B strong

C different

D evil

2 According to the legend, what proved that Arthur was the true king of England?

F He was able to pull out a special sword.

G Merlin remembered him as a boy.

H He knew all about his father the king.

J He was stronger than any other knight.

3 Which of the following is probably true?

A King Arthur may have really existed.

B Merlin really had magical powers.

C Guinevere was buried next to her king.

D Morgan Le Fay was really the sister of a king.

4 Which sentence is a *fact* from the passage?

F Merlin was a powerful magician with many talents.

G King Arthur never died and will return to England one day.

H Guinevere was the most beautiful woman in the land.

J The legend of King Arthur has been told for hundreds of years.

5 Which of the following will probably be true in the future?

   A King Arthur will return one day to England.

   B All the facts about King Arthur's court will be known.

   C People will continue to enjoy the legend of King Arthur.

   D Historians will discover what really happened to Guinevere.

6 The author probably wrote this passage to—

   F inform readers about the Legend of King Arthur

   G convince readers that the Legend of King Arthur was true

   H entertain readers with stories about King Arthur

   J explain why some legends became famous

7 According to the legend, which word best describes King Arthur?

   A thoughtful

   B angry

   C successful

   D foolish

8 The passage is *mostly* about—

   F King Arthur's childhood in England

   G whether or not Guinevere was a real person

   H how legends change over time

   J whether or not the Legend of King Arthur is true

9 A fairy tale is a make-believe story. Events in a fairy tale often cannot happen in real life. Which parts of the Arthur legend remind you of a fairy tale?

_____

_____

_____

_____

_____

_____

10 What did Geoffrey of Monmouth write about Merlin?

_____

_____

_____

_____

_____

_____

11   Do you believe that King Arthur was a real person? Did his Knights of the Round Table ever exist? Write an essay that states your opinion on the topic. Support your opinion with information from the passage. Use persuasive language in your essay.

Use a graphic organizer to plan your essay.

Write your essay on the lines below. If you need more space, continue writing on a separate sheet of paper.

_____

_____

_____

_____

_____

_____

_____

_____

_____

_____

_____

_____

_____

_____

_____

_____

DIRECTIONS: Read this story about a family who journey to California during the Gold Rush of 1849. Then answer questions 12 through 22. Darken the circle on the separate answer sheet or write your answer on the lines.

Joining the Forty-niners

Callie Everly climbed down from the wagon and shook her head in disbelief. A cloud of road dust made her cough and sneeze. She pulled her bonnet down to shade her blue eyes from the fierce sun.

Callie glanced around, but all she could see were a few shacks, some hitching posts, and a larger building called the General Store. "Papa, is this the whole town?"

Her father and older brother, John, led the team of horses over to the watering trough. Papa pushed back his hat and nodded. "It isn't much of a town yet, I guess. But I imagine that will change. With all these miners needing food and supplies, the town is sure to grow, honey."

Callie made a funny face and John laughed. "You didn't think it would be like Maryland, did you?" he asked.

They had left their snug home to try their luck as gold prospectors. After Mama died, there was nobody to stop Papa from leaving his job as a schoolteacher and heading West. Now, here they were in northern California, where a few flakes of gold from a place called Sutter's Mill had been discovered last year. In 1849, it seemed as if the whole world were heading West.

That night, the family put up their tents by the banks of a broad river. Their new neighbors were a mixed lot, some rough and loud, others quiet and determined. There were many more men than women and only a few children besides Callie and John. Callie listened carefully to the men talk of all of the gold that was yet to be found. One miner told of a mule that pulled a weed out of the river bank and uncovered gold in the dirt. When Callie fell asleep to the lapping of the river, she dreamed feverishly of finding gold chunks the size of her hand.

The next day, Callie had asked her father if she could look for gold too.

"I thought you wanted to be our cook and housekeeper," Papa said. Then he smiled and tugged at her braid. "But if you want to look for gold, we can certainly use an extra pair of hands."

Callie felt ridiculous when Papa handed her a pair of canvas pants and a boy's shirt. When she put them on, the only way to tell that she was a girl was by a dangling braid and her pale pink bonnet.

But after breakfast, Callie appreciated her unfeminine new outfit. She and John had to wade in the shallows of the river. Over and over, they dipped their pans, getting wet up to their knees. Her skirt would have been ruined. All around her, other gold-seekers stooped and panned, growing as wet and tired as she was.

All that morning, they panned for gold flakes in the river. They scooped up dirt and rocks in their pans, then swished them around. They barely paused to eat some salted meat and hard bread. By late afternoon, Callie's back ached from stooping. She was grateful to stop and fix the evening meal. Callie fell asleep almost as soon as she crawled into the tent.

Breakfast the next day was a hasty business so that they could return to the river. At lunch, Papa told them that a couple of other men would help him build a shack. "It will be more comfortable since we're going to spend the summer here on our claim," he explained.

Callie wondered if she could stand a whole summer of prospecting. She knew that her father was enthusiastic about their **venture.** Back home, he'd talked of little else for months. All he wanted was to stake a claim on a piece of land near Sacramento and get to work. If he found even one flake of gold, Henry Everly would remain by the side of this river for who knew how long. Callie said nothing, but silently resolved to spend less time panning and more time cooking. At least when she prepared a meal, she knew she was doing something worthwhile.

That evening, Will and Ben, two miners, joined them for supper. Will had left his family in Minnesota. He was a skilled carpenter. Ben was a young farmer who had turned over his property back home to his brother, in order to come out here.

"Sure, we'll get a shack up for you in no time," promised Will, while chewing a piece of salted pork. "It's the only sensible thing to do. When we get a thunderstorm, you'll want a roof over your heads."

For three days, the men worked on the shack, a one-room building with a single window. Papa hung a blanket across the room so that Callie could have privacy when she dressed. It was nothing like her old home, but it was much better than the tent.

venture: a risky undertaking

In return for their help, Papa promised to help Will and Ben operate their **cradle.** The cradle was much bigger than the pans they had used to search for gold. Three people had to work the cradle, rocking and sifting as water ran through it. And all the time, they were keeping their eyes peeled for gold.

Other prospectors had even more *sophisticated* mining tools. Some used a Long Tom, a shaft with a little basket at its end. Water and dirt went down the shaft, and the gold was supposed to get caught in the basket. Listening to the prospectors chat as they worked, Callie learned that up in the mountains, miners were tunneling into the mountainside and using special hoses that sprayed hard streams of water to wash dirt and gold down from the hilltops.

One day, Will showed Callie a leather pouch that he wore on a string around his neck. In it were three tiny gold nuggets and some yellow flakes. "I know there's more of this stuff around here. But even if I never find another speck of gold, I'm bringing this pouch home for my daughter. She's just about your age."

"When did you last see her?" wondered Callie. She wished Will's daughter were here so that she would have a friend.

"Oh, about eleven months ago," Will admitted. He looked sad for a moment. Then he shrugged, tucked the pouch back into his shirt, and strode off toward the river.

Callie sighed and kicked at a little clump of plants on the river bank. Soon it would be time to start cooking. She could tell by the angle of the sun that it was late afternoon. Then she held her breath: what was that, glinting among the greenish-gray weeds? She dropped to her knees and spread the weeds apart. A tiny, hard pebble shone brightly in her palm.

Callie ran down to the river. "Papa!" she cried, while stumbling over rocks and twigs, her boots growing muddier by the second. Her father froze. John also stopped working and stared her way. Callie opened her fingers and displayed the precious metal.

"Whoa, girl!" Papa exclaimed. "You've found the first gold nugget on the Everly claim!"

Papa, Callie, and John passed the little rock back and forth between them, talking and laughing excitedly. That night, Callie sewed the nugget into the lining of her skirt. As she drifted off to sleep she thought that one day they might have enough gold to fill a leather pouch.

cradle: a device used to wash dirt in order to find gold

12   How does Callie feel when she first sees the mining town?

    A   thrilled

    B   disappointed

    C   angry

    D   curious

13   This passage is an example of—

    F   an autobiography

    G   fiction

    H   a biography

    J   nonfiction

14   Most of this story takes place—

    A   in a newly built shed

    B   in Northern California

    C   in the woods in Maryland

    D   in a wagon out West

15   You can tell that the word *sophisticated* means—

    F   advanced

    G   huge

    H   rugged

    J   wonderful

16 Will and Ben help Callie's family—

    A find their own land

    B pan for gold with a new machine

    C build a shack to live in

    D cook dinner over a fire

17 Which is a *fact* from the story?

    F Gold was discovered at Sutter's Mill in 1848.

    G The gold prospectors were just wasting their time.

    H Callie's new clothes looked ridiculous on her.

    J John was better at panning for gold than Callie.

18 The boxes show some things that happen in the story.

Callie dreams of finding gold chunks the size of her hand.		Callie finds a gold nugget.
1	2	3

Which event belongs in Box 2?

    A Callie sees the mining town where her family will live.

    B Two miners join the family for dinner.

    C Callie sews gold into the lining of her skirt.

    D Papa leaves his job as a schoolteacher.

19 What is another good title for this story?

    F "An Overland Trip"

    G "Under California Skies"

    H "Catching Gold Fever"

    J "Callie Learns a Lesson"

20   Why does Callie change her mind and decide to pan for gold?

_____

_____

_____

_____

_____

_____

21   What can you tell about Callie from the story? What kind of person is she?

_____

_____

_____

_____

_____

_____

22 Imagine that you are Callie. Write a letter to a friend back home describing the experience of prospecting. Include details from the story that your reader might find interesting.

Use a graphic organizer to plan your letter.

Write your letter on the lines below. If you need more space, continue writing on a separate sheet of paper.

_____

_____

_____

_____

_____

_____

_____

_____

_____

_____

_____

_____

_____

_____

DIRECTIONS: Read these recipes for some snacks that are good for you. Then answer questions 23 through 33. Darken the circle on the separate answer sheet or write your answer on the lines.

Healthy Treats

Do you like sweets? Then you'll be happy to know that there are many easy recipes for delicious, healthy snacks and desserts. You don't have to load on the sugar when you try your hand at baking. Here a few great recipes to get you started in the kitchen.

Great Granola or Jam Bars

6 cups of rolled oats
1/2 cup of shredded coconut
1/2 cup of chopped nuts
1/2 cup of wheat germ, wheat flour, or oat bran
1/2 cup of powdered milk
1/4 cup of bee pollen
2/3 cup of cooking oil
2/3 cup of honey or maple syrup
1 teaspoon of vanilla extract or cinnamon
1 beaten egg
1/3 cup of milk

Preheat the oven to 350 degrees. Blend the dry ingredients together. Then add the liquid ingredients. Mix them well. Next, press the mixture firmly into 2 greased 10 x 15 inch cookie sheets. If you are making jam bars, spread the jam over 1/2 of the dry mixture, then put the other half on top. Bake at 350 degrees until slightly browned. Cut into bars right away. When they are cool, remove the bars from the tray with a spatula.

Cherry-Maple Crunch

3 cups of pitted sour cherries
I teaspoon of cornstarch
1/3 cup of maple syrup
1/2 cup of rolled oats
2 tablespoons of canola oil

Preheat the oven to 350 degrees. Grease a 9-inch pie plate with butter, margarine, or nonstick spray. Add the cherries. In a cup, combine the cornstarch and maple syrup. Pour over the cherries. Combine the oats and oil in a small bowl. Sprinkle this mixture over the cherries. Bake at 350 degrees for about 40 minutes.

Yummy Yogurt with Fresh Fruit

Note: The fruit in this recipe is just a suggestion. You can substitute any fruit you like.
    3 cups of plain yogurt
    I cup of fresh strawberries, cut in halves
    I or 2 medium-sized ripe peaches, sliced
    I ripe banana, sliced
    honey or maple syrup (optional)

Combine all the ingredients and chill in the refrigerator. Then eat and enjoy!

Very Healthy Oatmeal Cookies

This recipe makes about 12 large cookies or 24 small ones.
    I cup of oat flour
    I cup of whole wheat pastry flour
    I cup of rolled oats
    I teaspoon of baking powder
    I stick of butter
    1/2 cup of honey or brown rice syrup
    I egg
    1/3 cup of cow's milk, rice milk, or oat milk
    I teaspoon of vanilla extract
    brown sugar (optional)
    raisins and/or nuts (optional)

Preheat the oven to 350 degrees. Let the butter stand at room temperature until it is soft. Then cream the butter and honey or brown rice syrup together in a small bowl. Add a beaten egg, milk, and vanilla extract. In a medium-sized bowl, mix the pastry flour, oat flour, and baking powder. Combine all the ingredients and blend until the mixture is slightly sticky. Then add the rolled oats. Blend the mixture again. Finally, add the raisins and nuts, if you like your oatmeal cookies to have a little something extra. Drop the cookie dough onto the greased baking sheet. If you wish, you can sprinkle the cookies with brown sugar. Bake in the oven for about 12 minutes. The cookies are done when they are lightly browned on top. Let them cool, then remove cookies from the tray with a spatula.

23 What is the purpose of this passage?

  A To tell why sugar is bad for the body

  B To convince readers to eat healthy snacks

  C To compare healthy desserts to sugary sweets

  D To give readers some healthy snack recipes

24 For *most* of these recipes, you should start by—

  F mixing the dry ingredients

  G combining wet and dry ingredients

  H preheating the oven

  J greasing a baking sheet

25 How can you tell when the oatmeal cookies are done baking?

  A They will be light brown on top.

  B They will be soft and chewy.

  C They will be firm in the middle.

  D The edges will be crisp and dark.

26 What size pie plate should you use to bake Cherry-Maple Crunch?

  F 6 inches

  G 8 inches

  H 9 inches

  J 12 inches

27 The boxes show some steps in the preparation of Very Healthy Oatmeal Cookies.

Add a beaten egg, milk, and vanilla extract to the butter and honey mixture.		Combine all of the ingredients and blend.
1	2	3

Which step belongs in Box 2?

A Let butter stand at room temperature until it is soft.

B Add raisins and nuts.

C Mix the pastry flour, oat flour, and baking powder.

D Drop the cookie dough onto the greased baking sheet.

28 Which of these is an *opinion* in the selection?

F The recipe for Very Healthy Oatmeal Cookies makes about 12 large cookies.

G When they are cool, remove the granola bars from the tray with a spatula.

H You can substitute any fruit you like for the fruit in the recipe for Yummy Yogurt.

J You'll be happy to know there are many easy recipes for healthy snacks.

29 When making Great Granola or Jam Bars, what should you do *first*?

A Spread jam over half the dry mixture.

B Remove the bars from the tray with a spatula.

C Cut the mixture into bars that are about the same size.

D Press the mixture onto a cookie sheet.

30 How much milk do you need to make Very Healthy Oatmeal Cookies?

F 1/4 cup   **H** 1/2 cup

G 1/3 cup   **J** 1 cup

31 Which recipe is probably the easiest to make? Explain.

_____

_____

_____

_____

_____

_____

32 How would you describe the author's attitude toward healthy desserts?
Give reasons that support your answer.

_____

_____

_____

_____

_____

_____

33 Imagine that you have prepared one of the desserts described in the passage. Write an advertisement for this delicious treat. Use details from the selection in your advertisement along with your own persuasive language to convince people to sample your dessert.

Use a graphic organizer to plan your advertisement.

Write your advertisement on the lines below. If you need more space, continue writing on a separate sheet of paper.

_____

_____

_____

_____

_____

_____

_____

_____

_____

_____

_____

_____

_____

_____

DIRECTIONS: Read this poem about a windy day. Then answer questions 34 through 44. Darken the circle on the separate answer sheet or write your answer on the lines.

The Wind in a Frolic

by William Howitt

The wind one morning sprung up from sleep,
Saying, 'Now for a frolic! now for a leap!
Now for a mad-cap, galloping chase!
I'll make a *commotion* in every place!'
So it swept with a bustle right through a great town,
Creaking the signs, and scattering down
Shutters; and whisking, with merciless squalls,
Old women's bonnets and gingerbread stalls,
There never was heard a much **lustier shout,**
As the apples and oranges **trundled about;**
And the **urchins,** that stand with their thievish eyes
For ever on watch, ran off each with a prize.

Then it rushed like a monster on cottage and farm,
Striking their dwellers with sudden alarm;
And they ran out like bees in a midsummer swarm.
There were dames with their kerchiefs tied over their caps,
To see if their poultry was free from mishaps;
The turkeys they gobbled, the geese screamed aloud,
And the hens crept to roost in the terrified crowd;
There was rearing of ladders, and logs laying on
Where the thatch from the roof threatened soon to be gone.
But the wind had passed on, and had met in a lane,
With a schoolboy, who panted and struggled in vain;
For it tossed him, and twirled him, then passed, and he stood,
With his hat in a pool, and his shoe in the mud.

lustier shout: stronger or louder shout
trundled about: rolled around
urchins: children full of mischief

There was a poor man, **hoary** and old,
Cutting the heath on the **open wold**—
The strokes of his bill were faint and few,
Ere this frolicsome wind upon him blew;
But behind him, before him, about him it came,
And the breath seemed gone from his feeble frame;
So he sat him down with a muttering tone,
Saying, 'Plague on the wind! was the like ever known?
But nowadays every wind that blows
Tells one how weak an old man grows!'

But away went the wind in its holiday glee;
And now it was far on the billowy sea,
And the lordly ships felt its staggering blow,
And the little boats darted to and fro,
But lo! it was night, and it sank to rest,
On the sea-bird's rock, in the gleaming west,
Laughing to think, in its fearful fun,
How little of mischief it had done.

hoary: gray-haired
open wold: an open, rolling plain

34 What does the word *commotion* mean in the poem?

    A celebration

    B fury

    C discovery

    D friend

35 When it wakes up in the morning, the wind feels—

    F full of energy

    G very angry

    H a little tired

    J slightly confused

36 What does the wind do *first*?

    A Meet with an old man

    B Rock ships and boats at sea

    C Rush to a cottage and a farm

    D Meet with a schoolboy

37 The poem suggests that the wind—

    F likes to make trouble

    G thinks people are fond of it

    H is good for people and nature

    J is only dangerous to ships at sea

38 Which of the following *best* tells how most people in the poem feel about the wind?

   A "'Now for a frolic! now for a leap!"

   B "There never was heard a much lustier shout,"

   C "Plague on the wind! was the like ever known?"

   D "For ever on watch, ran off each with a prize."

39 How does the wind make the old man feel?

   F tough

   G frail

   H content

   J lost

40 What is this poem *mostly* about?

   A how it feels to be the wind

   B what animals think of the wind

   C how the wind affects people and places

   D what the wind does at sea

41 What do the geese do when the wind comes?

   F swarm like bees

   G huddle together

   H fall in the mud

   J scream out loud

42   How does the poet make the wind seem like a person?

_____

_____

_____

_____

_____

_____

43   What does the wind think it has accomplished at the end of the poem?

_____

_____

_____

_____

_____

_____

_____

44 Imagine that the old man in the poem has succeeded in capturing the wind in
        a huge sack. What do you think the man would do to the wind? Write a short
        narrative in which you tell what the old man might do to the wind.

Use a graphic organizer to plan your narrative.

Write your narrative on the lines below. If you need more space, continue writing on a separate sheet of paper.

_____

_____

_____

_____

_____

_____

_____

_____

_____

_____

_____

_____

_____

_____

_____

_____

_____

_____

DIRECTIONS: Read these two opposing arguments about the use of computers as teachers. Then answer questions 45 through 55. Darken the circle on the separate answer sheet or write your answer on the lines.

Computers Do the Teaching

You are about to begin your school day. You get out of bed when you feel rested. You have some breakfast, then decide whether you feel like getting dressed. It really doesn't matter if you keep your pajamas on—your teacher won't mind.

That's because your teacher is a computer.

Can computers really replace human teachers? Some people say yes. Computers provide individualized instruction to students. Each student learns at a pace that is right for him or her. Suppose your first assignment today is to complete a math worksheet. You answer the questions that appear on your computer screen. Then the computer scores the answers. Your electronic teacher directs you to correct your errors. You think you need more help, so you go to the next screen. There you find a page of hints to help you understand your errors.

Now it's time to do some reading. You download the story on your computer. After you read, you answer questions. Once again, the computer scores your responses, and you get extra help on the next screen.

You didn't have to bring books to school today. You didn't have to wait for other students to catch up during the lesson. You didn't have to interrupt others to ask your teacher to repeat some key information. You just clicked the mouse or pressed a key on your computer.

Long ago, a child learned in a one-room schoolhouse along with pupils of different ages. The teacher had to give different assignments to the children. Later, students were grouped in classrooms by age. Teachers presented the same material to the whole class. However, people learn differently. Educators tried to solve the problem by "tracking," putting students into regular, slow, and advanced classes. But tracking made many students feel uncomfortable. We tend to compare ourselves to others. When we think we are not doing as well as the next person, we feel unhappy with ourselves. So, some schools have stopped tracking students. Now what?

The computer does not need to compare one student to another. It just gives out and responds to information. A student can repeat an assignment as many times as necessary. This ensures success. And what is better than success in learning? It is time to rethink the classroom with rows of desks and a teacher at the front of the room. The world is changing fast. Education must change, too.

Computers Can't Teach

Think of the people who have made a difference in your life. Whom do you remember? Your parents, of course, and perhaps another family member or close friend. You also probably think of a few of your teachers. For example, your kindergarten teacher may have taught you to share with other children. Your second-grade teacher may have helped you discover the joys of reading. Perhaps your fourth-grade teacher took you on a field trip that helped you decide what you want to be when you grow up. Teachers can make a big difference in our lives.

Can a computer replace a teacher? Some experts believe that it can. They think computerized instruction is the way of the future. Computer programs promise to teach us all kinds of things. Some promise to teach us to chat in Spanish or to write an essay. Computer programs for young children promise to teach them the basics of reading, spelling, and math—in just an hour a day! Sound good? Sure, but something is missing from this package—the teacher and the students. Computer programs can teach and test students in many basic skills. However, there is more to a true education than reading words or adding up numbers. The classroom offers a rich, varied education for students. The ideas you exchange with others make education exciting. Your computer program may be able to tell you the "best" answer to a question about a story. But the computer doesn't let you share your thoughts with others. The computer cannot help you love learning. It cannot make learning personal. Only a real, live teacher can do that.

Think about it. Can a computer coach you through your first acting role in a school play? Can it help solve a problem between you and a classmate? Will it encourage you to be the best you can be? Before we choose computers for our teachers, we have to be able to answer questions like these. We need to think about the goals of education. There is more to learning than getting perfect test scores. A true education prepares students for a full, rewarding life.

45   In "Computers Do the Teaching," the author believes tracking students is a bad idea because—

   A   students do not score as well on tests

    B   students compare themselves to other students

   C   students are grouped by age instead of ability

   D   students learn in a one-room schoolhouse

46   Which is an *opinion* from "Computers Can't Teach"?

   F   Computers can score multiple-choice tests.

   G   Many people use computers for school or work.

   H   The computer is found in most classrooms.

   J   A computer cannot help shape a human life.

47   What is the main idea of "Computers Do the Teaching"?

   A   Most students enjoy learning at home.

   B   Computers save students a great deal of time.

   C   We need to find a better way to teach students.

   D   Computers can replace human teachers.

48   The author of "Computers Do the Teaching" included the information in the first paragraph to show that—

    F   learning with computers is easy

   G   computers make learning comfortable

   H   students do not learn in the classroom

   J   students are lazy when they are at home

49 In "Computers Can't Teach," the author says that learning from a human teacher is better than learning from a computer because a human teacher—

    A lets students work at their own pace

    B helps students get better test scores

    C makes learning more enjoyable

    D gives more homework assignments

50 Which is a *fact* from "Computers Do the Teaching"?

    F It is better not to lug books to school each day.

    G Some people think computers can replace teachers.

    H It is time for education to change.

    J The old way of learning is still the best way.

51 The purpose of "Computers Can't Teach" is to—

    A entertain readers with a story of a student learning at home

    B inform students about what it is like to learn from a computer

    C convince readers that human teachers are better than computers

    D teach readers the correct way to use a computer to learn

52 Both selections suggest that computers—

    F allow students to share thoughts with others

    G are not as good as real teachers

    H should replace teachers in the classroom

    J teach students some basic skills

53 List three advantages of using a computer to learn. Explain.

_____

_____

_____

_____

_____

_____

54 According to "Computers Do the Teaching," where would you go to get extra help when you're learning from a computer?

_____

_____

_____

_____

_____

_____

55 Write an essay stating whether you are for or against replacing human teachers with computers. In your persuasive essay, you may include some ideas from the selections as well as your own opinions and observations. Be sure to back up your point of view with sound reasons and convincing language.

Use a graphic organizer to plan your essay.

Write your essay on the lines below. If you need more space, continue writing on a separate sheet of paper.

_____

_____

_____

_____

_____

_____

_____

_____

_____

_____

_____

_____

_____

_____

Answer Sheet

TEST

1	Ⓐ Ⓑ Ⓒ Ⓓ	11	essay	21	short-answer	31	short-answer	41	Ⓕ Ⓖ Ⓗ Ⓙ	51	Ⓐ Ⓑ Ⓒ Ⓓ
2	Ⓕ Ⓖ Ⓗ Ⓙ	12	Ⓐ Ⓑ Ⓒ Ⓓ	22	essay	32	short-answer	42	short-answer	52	Ⓕ Ⓖ Ⓗ Ⓙ
3	Ⓐ Ⓑ Ⓒ Ⓓ	13	Ⓕ Ⓖ Ⓗ Ⓙ	23	Ⓐ Ⓑ Ⓒ Ⓓ	33	essay	43	short-answer	53	short-answer
4	Ⓕ Ⓖ Ⓗ Ⓙ	14	Ⓐ Ⓑ Ⓒ Ⓓ	24	Ⓕ Ⓖ Ⓗ Ⓙ	34	Ⓐ Ⓑ Ⓒ Ⓓ	44	essay	54	short-answer
5	Ⓐ Ⓑ Ⓒ Ⓓ	15	Ⓕ Ⓖ Ⓗ Ⓙ	25	Ⓐ Ⓑ Ⓒ Ⓓ	35	Ⓕ Ⓖ Ⓗ Ⓙ	45	Ⓐ Ⓑ Ⓒ Ⓓ	55	essay
6	Ⓕ Ⓖ Ⓗ Ⓙ	16	Ⓐ Ⓑ Ⓒ Ⓓ	26	Ⓕ Ⓖ Ⓗ Ⓙ	36	Ⓐ Ⓑ Ⓒ Ⓓ	46	Ⓕ Ⓖ Ⓗ Ⓙ		
7	Ⓐ Ⓑ Ⓒ Ⓓ	17	Ⓕ Ⓖ Ⓗ Ⓙ	27	Ⓐ Ⓑ Ⓒ Ⓓ	37	Ⓕ Ⓖ Ⓗ Ⓙ	47	Ⓐ Ⓑ Ⓒ Ⓓ		
8	Ⓕ Ⓖ Ⓗ Ⓙ	18	Ⓐ Ⓑ Ⓒ Ⓓ	28	Ⓕ Ⓖ Ⓗ Ⓙ	38	Ⓐ Ⓑ Ⓒ Ⓓ	48	Ⓕ Ⓖ Ⓗ Ⓙ		
9	short-answer	19	Ⓕ Ⓖ Ⓗ Ⓙ	29	Ⓐ Ⓑ Ⓒ Ⓓ	39	Ⓕ Ⓖ Ⓗ Ⓙ	49	Ⓐ Ⓑ Ⓒ Ⓓ		
10	short-answer	20	short-answer	30	Ⓕ Ⓖ Ⓗ Ⓙ	40	Ⓐ Ⓑ Ⓒ Ⓓ	50	Ⓕ Ⓖ Ⓗ Ⓙ		